COWLEY ROAD

Road Carnival 2004 !!

COWLEY ROAD

A HISTORY

Annie Skinner

SIGNAL BOOKS
Oxford

First published in 2005 by
Signal Books Limited
36 Minster Road
Oxford
OX4 1LY
www.signalbooks.co.uk

Reprinted and updated, 2008

A catalogue record for this book is available from the British Library

ISBN 1-904955-10-X Paper

Photographs: Catriona Davidson pp.iv, 1, 3, 15, 19, 21, 54, 55, 68, 71, 111, 121, 123, 124,
141; courtesy Oxfordshire County Council Photographic Archive pp.39, 51; author's collection pp.6, 25, 29, 48, 72, 79, 96, 105, 124, 127; courtesy www.atease.com p.137;
courtesy Maeve Bayton p.133; courtesy Daily Info, p.143 (the publisher would welcome
any further information regarding the author of the cartoon).
Cover Design: Baseline Arts
Cover Images: Keith Barnes; Catriona Davidson; Jeremy's (Oxford Stamp Centre); Annie
Skinner

Printed in India

CONTENTS

PREFACE AND ACKNOWLEDGEMENTS

Cowley Road is within half a mile of the centre of one of Britain's most celebrated cities, and literally a stone's throw from Oxford's High Street, described by Nikolaus Pevsner as "one of the world's great streets". A minute's walk takes you across the Plain and over Magdalen Bridge into what seems like another world.

If Oxford, the university and the city's architectural glories have been much written about, then Cowley Road has received little coverage. This street is a vital part of Oxford and has played an important role in its history and development, but its history is mostly untold. I wanted to correct this situation, not only because I have spent almost all my life in the area, but because Cowley Road seems to me to be interesting on two levels.

On the one hand, this street is highly typical of urban development in post-war Britain. Social changes in the areas of demography, migration, retailing and entertainment have taken place here as they have in any number of communities across the country. The decline of the corner shop and the rise of the mobile phone outlet is hardly a unique East Oxford phenomenon. So Cowley Road provides a snapshot of a wider process that has changed the face of almost every city and town in Britain.

On the other, Cowley Road is also highly unusual. Not only has it provided a physical link between the two worlds of Cowley, with its car manufacturing, and of the university, creating a particularly lively political climate, but it has also witnessed the coming together of migrants from around the world, students and other sometimes unconventional individuals in a uniquely tolerant community. This mix of ages, backgrounds and cultures is nowhere better celebrated than in the annual Cowley Road Carnival.

Although the road's history stretches back to medieval times, I have concentrated primarily on the last fifty or so years, since it is in the post-war period that Cowley Road has undergone its most spectacular social transformation. Its transition from a "respectable" working-class suburb into its present-day bohemian identity is the subject of this book.

It is important to capture this history in the context of time; otherwise it gets lost and forgotten. By drawing together people's memories, a poster collection, newspaper reports and official documents, I have attempted to create an original perspective of the transformation of Cowley Road over half a century. In a sense, this is "history from below", as remembered and told by people who have lived it, and as such it is often anecdotal rather than rigorously academic. But that is in keeping with its subject.

Many people have given up their time to help with this book and deserve thanks. I would particularly like to thank Malcolm Graham at the Centre for Oxfordshire Studies and all of the staff there for their patience and knowledge. Thanks must go to Virgil Clarke, John Stewart and Stan Taylor for reading through draft versions of this book and making helpful suggestions and comments. Extra thanks must go to Stan for the time he has spent in Cowley Road cafés with me, mulling over the local history of which he has been a mine of useful information. Others who have provided me with specialist information are as follows: Pat Clements has been an excellent source as an eye witness during the Eastwyke Farm Road saga; Anne Mobbs provided a wealth of information on community relations history, as did Ann Dummett and Sabir Hussain Mirza for today; Chris Griffin and Brian Tong for their overview on the role of the local constabulary; Maeve Bayton for the background to the Mistakes and Dick Page for his frank memories of his time as Ken Liversausage. I also wish to thank in particular Bill Heine, East Oxford Action, Oxfam and finally Jeremy's for help with old photographs of Cowley Road.

And thanks to the following people who have been so helpful and generous with their time: Richard Arridge, Jaime Báez, Dave Belden, Elise Benjamin Christine Birtwhistle, Cathy Booth, Zoe Brooks, Laurie and Jean Burrell, Jon Carpenter, John Clark, Ali and Pete Clements, Laurence Colbert, Ruth Conway, Robert Evans, Paul Foster, Ian Giles, Henrietta Gill, James

Hammond, Adrian Hopkins, Deborah Humphrey, Geno Humphrey, Tim Humphrey, Lorraine Jackson, Will Jarvis, Graham Jimpson, Andrew Koumi, Margaret and Peter Kearsey, Jane Kilpatrick, Mark Lynas, Bill Mackeith, David Manuel, Paul Morris, Roland Newman, Dave Newton, Mike Noble, Dave Norland, Dulcie Obhiozele, Claire Palmer, Mrs. Parchment, Graham Partridge, Kath Pateman, Mike Pateman, Nick Pile, Peter Purton, John Purves, Adam Romanis, Joe Ryan, Mr. Bagh Ali Sabir, Mr. Shauket Ali, Alwyn Samuel, Brian Stapley, Annie Sloan, Maurice Suckling, Anne Marie Sweeney, Alan Thornett, Diana Tickell, Mary Tinker, Chris Tree, and to everybody else who has contributed to this book.

Finally I would like to say thank you to James Ferguson of Signal Books for supporting the idea of this book. A very special thank you goes to my friends and family for putting up with me during this project, especially to my husband John Skinner who has given me much encouragement and support from beginning to end.

1

A CHANGING STREETSCAPE

"Cowley Road isn't Oxford, it's South London without the glamour," says the cynical narrator in Michael Dibdin's novel *Dirty Tricks*, featuring the East Oxford area. It is true that it looks like a street almost anywhere in suburban London or in any British city. With a hodge-podge of buildings, some very dull and some simply hideous, Cowley Road has few claims to architectural beauty, and those treasures it has are usually well hidden. But appearances can be deceptive.

The urban landscape changes as you walk along different sections of the road. If you enter Cowley Road from the city at the Plain and walk past the well-preserved Victorian cottages, there is a definite attractiveness. On one side of the road lights from an alternative therapy centre glow soothingly, while on the other side candles in the cafés radiate a welcoming invitation. The more "gentrified" western end of the street undoubtedly has its charms. But walking eastwards towards Cowley gives a different impression and the romanticism can fade, especially on a dreary, wet, cold February morning. Brutal modern buildings and relentless traffic do little to raise the spirits.

Ugly in parts it may be, but Cowley Road's outward appearance is only part of the story.

Cowley Road, officially also the B480, is a thoroughfare about a mile long and is one of the main streets leading into Oxford's city centre from its eastern suburbs. Leaving the centre and heading eastwards, it runs from the Plain, east of Magdalen Bridge to Cowley Marsh, where it turns into Oxford Road and continues to the former village of Cowley. Once a rural track, for much of the twentieth century it was often seen as little more than a link between the "dreaming spires" of the university city and the industry of Cowley and its car plant.

Today, however, Cowley Road has the reputation of a vibrant street, full of character, bohemian, multi-cultural, buzzing with political activity and interesting people. It is also judged by many who know it as tolerant, safe and musically vibrant.

The road's image has not always been so positive, so how and why did its present-day reputation occur? What were the influences behind this change in the street's self-perception?

A GALLOP THROUGH TIME

What we now know as Cowley Road once formed part of the main route from London to Oxford and over time has been known as Londonyshe (London) Street, Regia Via and Berrye Lane (1605). It crossed over a marsh and passed St. Bartholomew's Hospital, a leper hospital founded in the twelfth century. A track led from Oxford to the hospital and established an early link between the city and what would later become East Oxford, although this track did not follow the same course as present-day Cowley Road. From 1180 onwards, a pedestrian coming out of the city would have passed the Hospital of St. John Baptist on the left of Magdalen Bridge (East Bridge). The hospital, run by priests and sisters, was quite big, as it had been extended to include an infirmary, a hall for women and children and staff quarters. Magdalen College inherited the buildings in the fifteenth century and converted or demolished them.

Henry I had founded St. Bartholomew's Hospital for twelve lepers, near the Cowley Marsh, in 1126. The entrance to this site is opposite the former bingo hall. Leprosy was a contagious disease, and in the Middle Ages it was common practice to isolate lepers from their communities. Lepers were also treated as social pariahs in that period and needed somewhere to go to be cared for while suffering from the disease, which was particularly prevalent during the first part of the thirteenth century. St. Bartholomew's Chapel, built some 200 years later, was also part of the hospital. By the fifteenth century there were 200 leper houses in England, but St. Bartholomew's Hospital stopped admitting lepers at the beginning of that century and became an almshouse, then a hospital for plague patients, an alehouse, and then by the mid-seventeenth century, a farmhouse. During the cholera epidemic in 1832 an *ad hoc* Board of Health turned the hospital into a convalescent home.

In medieval times St. Clements Church and churchyard was sited on the Plain. The Plain, once a graveyard, is now the roundabout that links Cowley Road, Iffley Road and St. Clements *en route* to Oxford city centre. Beside St. Clements Church was St. Edmunds Well, where miracles were said to have happened, but these acts were banned twice by the Bishop of Lincoln in 1290 and 1304. St.

Clements Church was once a focal point of the area and was demolished in 1830. Most of the housing near the church was pulled down by 1777 when the city end of Iffley Road was built. This then replaced an older route which led into Cowley Road near Circus Street. St Clements was turnpiked in 1771, and a toll-house with gates on either side to charge travellers going in and out of the city was built in 1818. A local coach proprietor, Richard Costar lived on the present Magdalen College School site and had entrances to his property on both sides of the toll-gate. At the back of the ex-Cape of Good Hope (now The Pub Oxford), built in 1892, is a two-storey building, which was once a coach house and stable.

The Plain, named in 1830 after the church was demolished, was an open area surrounded by buildings. St. Clements toll-gate was demolished in 1874 and replaced by the Victoria Fountain in 1899. This monument was paid for by Mr. and Mrs. Morrell of Headington Hill Hall, who belonged to the brewing family that had been in the city since the eighteenth century, and was inaugurated by HRH Princess Louise.

The area between Cowley and Iffley Roads, known as Cowley Field, was mostly comprised of unenclosed and undeveloped open land. A local farming family, the Hursts, owned much of the land between James Street and Magdalen Road, which they sold off for development from 1861. There was at one time an orchard on the land between Marston Street and Stockmore Street. Once enclosure had taken place, rights of way across Cowley Field were restricted, plots were sold and the development of the road began. Part of the site of the bingo hall (previously the Regal cinema) was Cowley Common Land and was where, in the early nineteenth century, Magdalen Choir School played cricket. St. Clements and Cowley village were more developed communities than Cowley Road itself until the mid-nineteenth century.

When the workhouse in Wellington Square (Rats and Mice Hill) became inadequate for the city's poor, a new workhouse was created on Cowley Road in 1865. (At one stage consideration had been given to siting the workhouse in Park Town in North Oxford.) The mixed workhouse accommodated up to 330 inmates but was feared by many, as admission carried a great stigma. In 1930 the administration of the workhouse, which was by then known as Cowley Road Hospital and mainly used for the care of old people, was taken over by the Public Assistance Committee. In 1946 the hospital came under the jurisdiction of the National Health Service and was converted into a geriatric unit. Cowley Road Hospital was closed in 1981 and later demolished (this is now Manzil Way). Nazareth House, on the corner of Rectory Road, now James Mellon House (student accommodation), was built in 1875 and was once a Roman Catholic orphanage and old people's home. Nazareth House stopped functioning as an old people's home in 1994.

Cowley Road really came into its own in the mid-nineteenth century when the area was developed as a suburb of the city. Although Oxford University had been a major landowner in the city for centuries, at this time the institution did not exert a monopoly in East Oxford. The suburb was instead developed by a number of new landowners from the 1850s onwards, and the community developed from then on, albeit on a piecemeal basis. The National Freehold Land Society (NFLS), founded in 1849, had Liberal backing and was one of the first building societies. Political motives lay behind its activities, as providing land and freehold plots undoubtedly increased the voting population. The Conservative Land Society was formed in 1852, effectively providing political opposition. Regardless of the political implications, these societies provided cheap building plots and encouraged home ownership among working men. Alma Place was one of the first NFLS developments in 1852. Marston Street was developed in 1853 and Temple and Stockmore Streets in 1856. Others followed later. The Oxford Industrial and Provident Land and Building Society laid out Southfield Road and Divinity Road in 1891. Meanwhile, building continued along Cowley Road at different paces.

One of the outcomes of varied landowners and a gradual process of development is that each street had, and continues to have, its own individuality and character. Another feature of East Oxford is that its gradual development allowed for changing styles in house building, from the mid-nineteenth century to modern homes built today. Houses ranged from small terraced cottages to grander detached dwellings, differing markedly from street to street. In his books on St. Clements and East Oxford, Malcolm Graham takes the reader on a journey through the area. He identifies buildings of particular significance and explains their place in local history. For example, many houses were originally built for residential use but were later converted for commercial use and some of these are described in his books. Frank Courtenay-Thompson has written an illuminating case history of Marston Street in his book *Just by Chance*, which takes a closer look at the many influences on a local street's history.

Houses were purchased by building societies or estate agents and duly sold. Owners had the option of renting out their homes, which some did. Lodging houses were also quite common in the area during the first half of the twentieth century. Many houses were suitable for this purpose, and it was not unusual for people to take in lodgers.

As the suburb expanded, influenced by rural migration, shopping facilities evolved. It was not unusual to have a shop in a side street and some had several. Even so, it is clear that Cowley Road developed as the central street for the provision of services, and as an arterial road it was logical that it should serve as the main commercial centre. Residents determined demand for services. Schools, health services and churches were established alongside building societies, lawyers, accountants and general and specialist shops for the growing community.

Cowley Road, Oxford

ESSENTIAL SERVICES

St. Clements parish included part of Cowley Road (from Divinity Road to the Plain), and was incorporated into the City of Oxford in 1835 under the Municipal Corporations Act. The Paving Commission, established in 1771, was responsible for cleaning the city streets and the removal of nuisances. Following the 1832 cholera epidemic, when St. Clements suffered a third of all deaths in Oxford, drinking water was brought from Headington to pumps at the end of each street in 1849. Drainage did not begin to appear until after 1854.

By this time Cowley Road had started to be developed and some parts of the area, particularly the main road from the Plain to Magdalen Road, were paved, but the side streets took longer. Rubbish collection in East Oxford was considered by some to be second-rate compared to the service in North Oxford. In his book *Images of Victorian Oxford*, Malcolm Graham reproduces correspondence from an East Ward ratepayer complaining in 1891 to the town clerk about the allegedly preferential treatment given to North Ward, and suggests that some services were prioritized in more prosperous and influential areas such as North Oxford. The letter describes the state of the street and inadequate collection in the area and continues: "but as far as I know, the working classes of the East, West and South Wards would be quite as ready to give a small present at the time which will soon be here now as their neighbours in the north of Oxford, if the same attention were shown them…" The Local Board was responsible for providing essential services in the city from 1865 until a new Council was established in 1889. Since then legislation and responsibilities have changed accordingly, notably with the establishment of the National Health Service in 1946, and Oxfordshire County Council's taking over of education and highways in 1974.

The Oxford Electric Company was formed in 1890. In the early days changing over to electricity was expensive for many in poorer areas of the town, but gradually during the first half of the twentieth century residents in the area began to have access to electricity. Upon nationalization in 1948, Oxford was served by the Southern Electricity Board. A local depot was set up in Marston Street. The Oxford Gas Company was formed in 1818, and similarly after nationalization became part of the Southern Gas Board. Telephones, also an expensive service, came to Oxford in 1878, but in East Oxford this facility was initially confined to people in commercial occupations.

THE "RESPECTABLE" WORKING CLASS

Earlier in the twentieth century the people living on or near Cowley Road were from all sorts of backgrounds. There was a mixture of house owners and tenants, and among these were many college servants and local tradespeople. Later, workers from Morris Motors, the factory which produced the first cars in Cowley in 1913, settled here, as did other workers from developing industries in the area. Robert Waller, who has written on Oxford's political history, observes that East Oxford was judged to be "a rather conservative, deferential, stable community of college servants and the so-called 'respectable' working class." Another writer on Oxford's history, Richard Whiting, supports this view and suggests that the area was populated by a mixture of skilled and unskilled workers and among them a significant number of car workers.

Oxford University had dominated the employment market in the city until the early 1920s and the establishment of the Morris Motor works in Cowley. After this the occupational structure of the population changed as a new group of semi-skilled workers, who could earn as much as traditional craftsman, evolved. Many benefits to the city arose from the expansion of the car industry, which provided a major source of employment in competition with the university, and other traditional local industries. Florence Park estate was built in 1933 for the increasing numbers employed at the factory. Many Welsh workers who had come to Oxford to find work at the factory moved to the estate, which was known as "Little Wales". The estate was developed by Norman Moss, who also donated a 21-acre park to the city. Florence Park and the estate were named after his sister Florence. Employment in Oxford was relatively stable from 1945 to 1960, with few people on the dole.

Census statistics from 1951 give a more detailed impression of the people who lived in the Cowley Road area. Over half of the male population over 16 years of age came from social class III (Registrar General's social class index skilled non-manual and manual). A further 25 per cent of the community came from classes IV (semi-skilled) and V (unskilled). In fact, only three per cent of the male population were judged to belong to social class I. There were a fair amount of older people in the neighbourhood, but the majority were younger and half of the community were married.

Further information from the census gives an insight into the social conditions that people experienced during the 1950s. Of the 4,157 households in the area 46 per cent had no fixed bath; a sink was shared or absent, and a water closet was shared or absent for seventeen per cent of the households; and 37 per cent had exclusive use of piped water, cooking stove, kitchen sink, water closet and fixed bath. The picture painted shows that, in general, East Oxford was a relatively poor area of the city and that for nearly half of the households domestic and sanitary conditions were limited. This picture was not, of course, unique to East Oxford, as many British homes had no bathroom. What we can see, however, is that the East Oxford community in the 1950s was stable and generally conservative, a law-abiding neighbourhood with no conspicuous social problems.

Cowley Road in 1950 was, broadly speaking, similar to how it had been in the 1930s and 1940s. The country had been through the Depression and the Second World War, and much energy had been used up simply surviving these difficult times. Social trends had not yet had time to change because of the impact of wartime shortages and economic crisis, and shops and businesses were rudimentary in terms of choice and service. This was partly due to the fact that rationing was still in process and in general there was an atmosphere of austerity.

SIGNS OF CHANGE

In the early 1950s there was limited evidence of ethnic minorities in the community. James Hammond was one of the first black officers in the United States Air Force in charge of mixed-race troops and was posted at one of the bases in 1952. He, his wife and baby lived on Cowley Road in 1952. He talks of his experience of being the only black family in the neighbourhood:

> We'd take Kevin for a walk in the neighbourhood and I love this... we were out walking and people would come out and look at us and look at Kevin and say "what a pretty little piccaninny"... and piccaninny was offensive but I took it to mean they were being complimentary, not being degrading or vicious or racist—but I just took it that they were being nice and they didn't realize that piccaninny could be offensive to us. So I was offended but yet not offended... As far as I know at that time, as black Americans we were called coloured people and they'd not seen us before and everybody would come over and look at us... We were just something they had not seen before and they were I guess just trying to get a new experience of people that looked like they'd not seen before.

James Hammond's recollections remind us how the community was predominately white in those days, and how unusual it was to see people from other cultures in the area. It also shows us how our language reflected stereotypes and ignorance. It was not long after this, however, that people from the West Indies came to Oxford, as during the 1950s and early 1960s there was a large increase in immigration to Britain from the Caribbean. The post-war growth in industrial production had actually created severe labour shortages and, in general, Britons were reluctant to take on some of the low-paid shift-work jobs. Consequently, people from the West Indies arrived in Britain to take on these jobs. In December 1954 a group of men came over from Jamaica to live in Oxford and were taken on at the City of Oxford Motor Services. This event was reported in the *Oxford Times*. Part of the interest in the story was that there had been problems with the bus service, and it was hoped that the new recruits would help alleviate these difficulties. One other interesting aspect of the story is that the bus workers' trade union, the Transport and General Workers' Union, seriously took up the issue of the new recruits. The union 5/59 branch met from 12 midnight till 2.45 am and concluded that the decision to employ the new staff on the same conditions as existing workers was in line with union policy, which was opposed to any colour bar in the bus-passenger service. (Incidentally, the bus service did not seem to improve and the debate continued.) In March 1955, the Oxford City Watch Committee, precursor to the police committee, reported that up to fifty more West Indians were to be employed on the buses and that this "should ease the problem."

Although the new arrivals from the West Indies were originally accommodated at the bus company's hostel on Cowley Road, more immigrants arrived who did not work at the bus company. Many West Indians settled in the Cowley Road area, as some of the houses had become lodging houses, but they often lived in inadequate accommodation, especially for families. Some West Indian men had come over to the UK alone, but their families came later. Gradually the West Indian community increased and a whole new culture opened up. One of the first contributions to the area was the introduction of different foods in local shops. There were not immediate changes, but after a while shops began to cater for the changing community's culinary needs. One of the first shops in the 1960s to stock Caribbean foods was a delicatessen known as Eddie's, on the corner of Bullingdon Road. This shop was widely welcomed, as it increased the variety of produce available to residents.

During the late 1950s and 1960s more people from the Caribbean came to live in the Cowley Road area. Despite a general acceptance of the newcomers, there was inevitably some overt racism in the area, and newcomers experienced various forms of hostility. Chapter 4 highlights a particular case of discrimination and the community response to it. In the meantime, some people from the Caribbean community began to move out of the area to places like Blackbird Leys, where a new housing development offered more suitable accommodation for families. But a considerable number of people from the Caribbean still remained in the neighbourhood. As the African-Caribbean community grew, the need for a social centre became apparent. Members of the community were meeting in each other's houses, but with growing numbers this became impractical.

Eventually, the Caribbean Sunrise Club was established by members of the Caribbean community in 1973. Initially the premises were shared with the other organizations including the East Oxford Community Association, which moved to premises in Princes Street in 1975. The building that housed the club was an old school on Cowley Road, now the site of Boots chemists. It was in a dilapidated condition, and members did their best to make it feel homely by painting and decorating. Regular social events were held there, and people remember going to these with their families. Second-generation members of the Caribbean community recall going to the club as small children and have fond memories of the place. It was used as a gathering place, where people played dominoes, listened to music and generally met with others. Saturday nights were the sessions for "grown-ups" and Sundays were for teenagers and families. There were also special occasions such as Jamaican Independence Day when bigger events were organized. The *Oxford Times* reported on this event in 1975, as this was apparently the first time that the community had celebrated Independence Day since 1963, as previously there were no suitable premises, and there were high hopes that this was to be an annual celebration.

The Caribbean Sunrise Club was a colourful part of the Cowley Road landscape for a relatively brief period of time. When the site was sold by the City Council in 1976 and redeveloped as premises for businesses and flats, the club moved to Paradise Square for a few years, while Roots, a club established by and for young black people, was based at South Oxford Middle School. Both these organizations have since been disbanded, but the African-Caribbean Community Action Network continues to campaign for a centre. Other projects had been based at the former school building, and some people believed that the City Council had made commitments for future community use of the site. As a result, there was acrimonious correspondence in the *Oxford Times* about the alleged reneging by the Council.

ASIAN MIGRATION

Immigrants from the Indian subcontinent also came to live in the UK, but in the late 1950s were fewer in number and mostly lived in other areas of the city, especially Jericho and West Oxford. The majority in Oxford came from Pakistan, but there were also significant minorities from India and later Bangladesh. Many came to join others from the same village and arrived without their wives and children. Like migrants from the Caribbean, Pakistani men filled a gap in the employment market and took on semi-skilled and unskilled jobs. Quite a few Pakistani men were able to get work in the Bicester Ministry of Defence establishment and the paper mills in Wolvercote and Sandford. Getting work at the car factory, however, was virtually impossible, as there was an unofficial colour bar in operation. It took the intervention of the Oxford Committee for Racial Integration and trade union involvement before more West Indians and Pakistanis were employed at the factory after 1965, but usually in unskilled positions. Meanwhile, as "Indian" restaurants became more popular, several opened in the city and provided other employment. Language was also a problem for newcomers who were dependent on their more experienced compatriots. Initially, the community founded a mosque in a restaurant in Walton Street but in 1965 one was opened in Bath Street in St. Clements.

More Pakistanis moved over to East Oxford in the late 1960s, as the community increased and more accommodation was needed. Wives and children came to live in the UK about this time, and the lodging houses that the men had been living in were inadequate for families. Alison Shaw's study, *The Pakistani Community in Oxford*, addresses the reasons why wives and children came to Britain. Among those cited were the reuniting of husbands and wives and the re-establishment of the community (once re-united the husbands did not then have "bachelor status"). Wives and children arriving in the city reinforced a commitment to staying here, and many considered that there were better prospects for their families than in Pakistan. Houses in East Oxford were generally cheaper than elsewhere in the city and although they often had outside toilets and no bathrooms, council grants were available for modernization. As the Asian community developed in East Oxford, local stores started to change and introduced more "exotic" products, including groceries, clothes and other goods from the subcontinent. Another spin-off was the proliferation of new restaurants in Cowley Road, adding further choices to the area. Cowley Road Hospital was demolished by 1986, and the old chapel site was turned into the Asian Cultural Centre. The centre has been used for projects in the community ranging from play schemes to older people's clubs and is a positive social asset.

Schools and playgroups had to respond to the cultural additions to the neighbourhood. Cowley St. John Playgroup was based behind the East Oxford Community Centre and was one of the first local multi-racial playgroups, beginning in 1970. Its organizers were attuned to the needs of children from different cultural backgrounds and actively encouraged parents from different communities to send their children to the playgroup. Those involved in the playgroup movement belonged to the Pre-Playgroup Association, where wider educational issues and the needs of ethnic minorities were flagged up. Once in mainstream schooling, different issues were raised by children of different ethnic backgrounds, and specialist advisors were eventually introduced to respond to specific educational needs. The Oxford Committee for Community Relations also started to run Saturday Schools for children from the ethnic communities, as evidence started to suggest that they were sometimes not doing well at school and parents became concerned about their education. The Saturday Schools also provided cultural identity for the children but folded in the mid-1980s.

East Oxford also became home to people from other countries such as Italians, Poles, Greeks, Turks, Russians and Irish. By the mid-1960s there was an interesting combination of cultures in the area. Gradually shops and businesses came to represent aspects of these cultures and enhanced the ambiance of the road. One businessman is proud to say that in his block of shops and businesses every owner comes from a different country of origin. In recent years the biggest influx of migrants has come from Eastern Europe, and Poland in particular.

Oxford has traditionally been welcoming to refugees, and today Cowley Road continues this tradition and is home to Asylum Welcome at no. 276. Asylum Welcome was set up in 1996 by local people in response to the growing needs of refugees and asylum seekers. Individuals who had been visiting detainees at Campsfield Immigration Detention Centre, just outside Oxford, were alerted to the needs of those who were released, ranging from help in accessing medical services to finding accommodation. Asylum Welcome amalgamated with an existing organization, Refugees in Oxford. Refugees have come from countries that have been, or are, in conflict such as Uganda, Iraq, Afghanistan and Kosovo. Many of the refugees feel comfortable in the Cowley Road environment, where a multi-cultural atmosphere enables them to feel less conspicuous.

PROPERTY BOOMS

There was a general move towards home ownership in the 1960s, when property was cheap in East Oxford. There was, in fact, a shortage of purchasable property in the city as a whole as building societies were not keen to give mortgages on older properties and there was a scarcity of newer homes. But Cowley Road underwent something of a boom, as reported in the *Oxford Times* in August 1959.

> Prices of second-hand houses rocketed in Oxford during the past 10 months by as much as 10% to reach a post-war peak. Two reasons for this are given: Government improvement grants have made it possible for older houses to be modernised, and a big scarcity of post-war houses in the area with a growing demand for them.
>
> Older terrace houses are now fetching record prices. Agents are now finding that properties such as those off the Cowley Road may fetch up to £1,400 whereas nothing more than £1,250 could be expected a few months ago. Mr C D Boyce, Manager of Oxford Cooperative

Permanent Building Society, thinks government improvement grants for pre-1919 houses have played a big part... A family terrace house "straight off the one street which would normally fetch £1,200 might now be sold for £1,500-£1,600—provided it is brought up to date with a grant."

Charles O Wilkins from E Gordon Hudson Ltd said "I don't think Oxford is a fair comparison with the rest of the country. But certainly, in Oxford, the prices of new houses have reached a peak.

Similar houses in Risinghurst were on the market for £2,850 and in Rose Hill for £3,100. In general, house prices were dependent on the size and condition of the property, and some East Oxford properties sold for more.

An added bonus was the fact that the City Council offered Home Improvement Grants to help owner-occupiers improve their homes in selected streets. These grants arose from a government initiative to improve the quality of housing in the country. The most obvious target involved modernizing sanitary facilities, as many homes were still without bathrooms. In June 1953 at the East Ward Labour Party meeting attention was drawn to the lack of sanitary amenities in the area. A resolution was sent to the City Council requesting it to give careful consideration to the urgent need for "slipper baths", i.e. public baths, in the ward. A scheme to provide wash houses and baths for the "industrious classes" had been launched in 1850. Oxford Corporation opened baths in 1923 in Paradise Square, while slipper baths and swimming baths were in Merton Street (leased from the university).

Hundreds of houses in the area were said to have no bathrooms, and the 1953 resolution requested the installation of baths at Catherine Street as this facility would save many factory workers the journey to Paradise Square for a bath. Slipper baths were available in Catherine Street from 1954, and many considered a weekly bath there part of a normal routine. They were closed by the City Council in 1978 due to falling demand.

One home owner, who purchased his home later, explains how building societies and the Council changed their attitudes towards the purchase of older properties in the area:

At that time building societies were very conservative about the type of property they would lend money on and they didn't like older property, pre- 1930s really—they would only give a 75% mortgage. When we bought our house [in 1966] the City Council were offering mortgages for pre-1919 property because there was such a huge stock of Edwardian property in Oxford in this area that was in reasonable shape, and they wanted to contribute to the needs of people, so they were giving a 95% mortgage and we had a 95% mortgage on our house, and that was built in 1906. That was a big boost to this type of property—and now to think that an Edwardian terraced house would have been a difficult house to buy because building societies regarded them as old dodgy property—it is amazing, isn't it? Everybody wants to live in them now!

When people were asked why they moved here in the 1960s and early 1970s, one of the main reasons was the cheap property. Although there was effectively a planning blight in the area (see Chapter 2), new home owners were not aware of this, nor of the fact that there were plans for an inner-city relief road to run through the area.

Long-term residents remember that the Cowley Road area had a very static population in the 1960s and early 1970s. One couple who moved to East Oxford in the mid-1960s recall that there were not many families living in their area then, but that many elderly widows lived in the street and many of them took in lodgers. Often lodgers would stay on and set up home in the area. Over time more families moved into the area around this time. Another couple who lived in Hurst Street remember that when their elderly neighbour died in the early 1970s and the house was sold, the new owners converted it for multi-occupation. They feel that this was symptomatic of the widespread move towards multi-occupation.

STUDENTS ARRIVE

Not surprisingly, there were few students living in the area in the 1950s and early 1960s. This is because the university provided accommodation for most of its students and was just beginning to expand, and there was as yet no Oxford Brookes University. At the end of the 1960s, plans were well under way to create Oxford Polytechnic (previously the Oxford College of Technology), and the university and its colleges were starting to build student accommodation in the area, notably in Iffley Road and St. Clements. By the early 1970s there were 1,900 students at Oxford Polytechnic and the plan was to increase this number to 4,000. Oxford University also had plans to increase its number of students, and it was predicted that by 1980 the combined student population would reach 17,000.

From the mid-1970s onwards an increasing number of students were living in East Oxford, as property was cheap. Most lived in former family homes, converted into multi-occupation rented accommodation. This trend caused concern to organizations such as Shelter, which considered that students were occupying family accommodation and contributing to homelessness in Oxford. Meanwhile, property booms and the recession in the 1980s created a shift in the make-up of the population in East Oxford, as it remained a relatively cheap area. Around this time, parents started to buy property for their children to live in while they studied at university.

Many students remained in the Cowley Road area after completing their courses, as they felt it was a good place to live. Not only was property good value, but there was easy access to the main employment providers—the polytechnic and university and the hospitals—as well as to the town centre and commuter services, and this appealed to new families. East Oxford was fast becoming an attractive place to live for many different people, therefore contributing to its diverse culture and political interests.

TODAY'S POPULATION

It is difficult to make direct comparisons between the population now and in the past, partly because ward boundaries have moved and also because the nature of census data has now changed. However, by using 2001 census data for St. Mary's Ward an idea of changes over fifty years can be seen. St. Mary's Ward is effectively a triangle of streets, stretching from the Plain to Magdalen Road, and includes one side of Cowley Road, one of Iffley Road and the streets in between, with a total population of 5,040. The 2001 census reveals that 10.4 per cent of residents were aged 16 years and under; 49.2 per cent were aged between 20 and 29; and 2.9 per cent were aged over 75 years. Furthermore, 42.8 per cent were full-time students, compared with a general average of 5.51 per cent for the city as a whole. Class and social distinctions are more difficult to ascertain. Other criteria are available that can be used to make some evaluation; for example, 48.9 per cent of the population were considered to be economically active, 2.3 per cent were unemployed, and 38.9 per cent had a degree or higher qualification—a figure fractionally higher than the city overall. There were 36.4 per cent of home owners, and 49.1 per cent rented their homes in the private sector. Although predominately white, St. Mary's Ward has a higher level of mixed ethnic groups than the city average, with the largest ethnic group being the Pakistani community. It has been said that some years ago over 29 different languages were spoken by children at the local First School. St. Clements Ward had similar statistics to those of St Mary's. (National Statistics website: www.statistics.gov.uk)

The statistics show that nearly half the residents in the area are under thirty, that there is a small elderly population, and that almost half of the population are working. What is particularly evident, moreover, is that students now occupy a large part of the area; that there are fewer older people living in the district; that there is a high demand for rented accommodation; and that there is a diverse ethnic composition.

In February 2005, a three bedroom semi-detached house advertised for sale in Risinghurst was valued at £205,000, while a similar house in Rose Hill was for sale at £250,000. A three bedroom terraced house in East Oxford, meanwhile, was on the market for £280,000. Even though this is a simple comparison, it reflects the turnaround of house prices in the city in relation to those in the 1950s. Now it is considered fashionable to live in the area, and houses are more expensive than in the areas that were considered more desirable in the 1950s.

RELIGION ON THE ROAD

One of the most influential figures in the area's history was undoubtedly Richard Meux Benson, (1824-1915), known as Father Benson, as he played an important role in the development of Cowley Road. He was the vicar of Cowley parish in 1850 and while there was instrumental in forming the parish of Cowley St. John in 1868. Father Benson became the first vicar of this expanding parish in 1869. Before St. Mary and St John Church in Cowley Road was built, parishioners congregated in a specially constructed temporary church in Stockmore Street, which Father Benson had organized. This was known as the "Iron Church" and was used by parishioners for quite a few years until the new church was ready. St. Mary and St. John Church had the foundation stone laid in 1875 and was consecrated in 1883.

Father Benson was strongly influenced by the Oxford Movement, a religious group keen to follow some of the original teachings of the Catholic Church under the Anglican doctrine. John Henry Newman, a Fellow of Oriel and later Vicar of St. Mary's, the University Church, along with Keble and others, was one of the founder members of the Oxford Movement in 1833. Following his further doctrinal interpretations which caused uproar in the university, Newman was denounced as a traitor and left the Movement. He retired to Littlemore in 1841 and continued his religious studies, was ordained as a priest in Rome and made a cardinal in 1879.

All this was happening whilst Father Benson was developing his parishes. During his time as vicar of Cowley parish he founded the Society of St. John the Evangelist, a congregation of mission priests that moved into the mission house in Marston Street in 1868. A church was built in the grounds, and they became known locally as the Cowley Fathers and were regularly seen in the area. Father Benson was also influential in founding schools in the area, and the Society ran a successful boys' club in Marston Street.

In 1950 there were three main churches on Cowley Road: these were Methodist, Congregationalist and Anglican, and there was also the medieval St. Bartholomew's Chapel. The chapel is still used today for occasional services, concerts and art exhibitions.

St. Mary and St. John Church was a flourishing parish church, and many activities went on there. A festival of the parish was commemorated at the church in May 1962 when the mayor and members of the City Council went in state to the church service. The service was attended by representatives of the churches, religious community and other organizations in the large parish, including the scout and guide groups. Parishioners had raised money for two seats as memorials to two well-known former parishioners, Mr. Frank Parker and Mr. Matt Gray. Both were East Oxford men who had lived all their lives in the parish. These seats were unveiled after the service. Regular concerts were held for fund-raising purposes, especially for the organ.

Nowadays the church has a regular congregation that encompasses a wide section of the community. Attached to the church is a two-acre Victorian graveyard. The burial ground, one of Father Benson's contributions to the area, is now closed for burials. There is a memorial to Father Benson in the churchyard. An ongoing project involving local volunteers has been working to

improve the graveyard since 2000. Since then the graveyard has become more accessible to the community as walkways have been improved and the area is now a pleasant environment to enjoy. A Heritage Lottery grant has recently funded an educational graveyard trail (www.ssmjchurchyard.org.uk).

The Congregationalist Church was built in May 1880 on the corner of James Street and Cowley Road (the site is now home to Oxfordshire Social Services). It was constructed to replace a smaller church that had been used for about ten years. Previously the Congregationalists had met in a warehouse. Before the Second World War this church had one of the first woman ministers of congregational union, Rev. Constance Coltman. She was married to Rev. Claude Coltman, who was in charge of the church at the time.

The church moved to Blackbird Leys in 1962 and at that time had "127 members, with a minister, a deaconate and a fully organised church life with considerable assets." Although there was another Congregationalist Church in Oxford, the *Oxford Times* described the church on Cowley Road as "one of the best known of Oxford's free churches" over the preceding eighty years. The last service was in April 1962. Money raised from the sale of the site was used to build the new church at Blackbird Leys.

This Cowley Road church stood next to the Congregationalist Hall, which provided a welcome venue for events such as annual flower shows and other general community occasions not associated with the church. Apparently it was widely used by the Liberal Club, and was obviously a popular resource that combined the spiritual with community use. Pleasant Sunday Afternoons (PSAs) were held there for women on Sundays. In October 1952 the PSA celebrated a Diamond Jubilee in the Congregationalist Hall. One resident remembers taking her grandmother to these events regularly when she was a youngster. She recalls it as a peculiar church, and describes it as "being down in a well... tiered seats with an altar at the bottom... a nice building but with railings around the outside. The hall was next door and quite big and used for social events."

Cowley Road Methodist Church was established in 1904 and came about because the existing chapel in William Street (now Tyndale Road) was inadequate for the growing number of Methodists in the area. One of the characteristics of this church is that people from different cultures attend services. When immigrants from the Caribbean arrived in the UK, they were very keen to keep up with their religious beliefs, but many felt that they were not accepted into most mainstream churches. Some consider that this was partly because their way of worship was more open than and different from traditional English styles of worship. In order to satisfy their spiritual needs some members of the Caribbean community started their own prayer groups in homes. As these became bigger they then had to move to halls, and new prayer groups such as the New Testament Church of God were established.

At the same time, many African-Caribbean people did attend the Cowley Road Methodist Church and took their children to services. Members of the congregation felt that they were very much integrated into the church and enjoyed their time of worship. Joe Gibbon, who was the minister of the church from 1965 to 1972, was very active in a protest against racial discrimination at a local hairdresser in 1967. He was arrested along with other local dignitaries (see p.83). Since 1967 Punjabi Christians have been incorporated into the church, a consequence of a growing number of Christians from the Punjab settling in the area.

In September 2004 the church held its centenary celebrations and published a book to celebrate this milestone. The book gives a detailed history of the church.

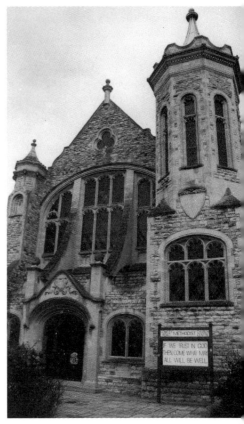

Exciting events took place at the Regal cinema (more recently the bingo hall) during June 1967. Billy Graham, the famous American evangelist, was in Britain preaching and from 23 June to 1 July live recordings of his services from Earls Court were shown on closed circuit TV at the cinema in the evenings. Entrance to the events was free. A great many people attended these screenings, according to reports in the *Oxford Times*, with a total of 13,165 attending (an average of 1,500 at each of the nine screenings). The total cost amounted £4,500 (of which £3,900 was raised by donations). An address was made by the Bishop of Oxford at the Regal commending those who made a profession of faith. But a local cleric, Sid Hinkes, criticised Dr. Graham for having "no public view on the Vietnam War", which he considered a cowardly way of saying nothing about the issue of the day. This criticism was made when he spoke at public forum organized by Thame District Peace Committee.

The Pentecostal Church met at the Coop Hall for three years from 1968, until their church was ready in Stockmore Street.

It is probably accurate to say that, in general, people do not visit the established church as often now as they did in the 1950s. Andrew Rosen provides interesting figures on church attendance compared with Sunday shoppers in *The Transformation of British Life 1950-2000*. Apparently eleven million people go shopping each Sunday and one million attend church. Alternative religions such as Buddhism have meanwhile grown in popularity. Regardless of this trend, Cowley Road's Methodist Church and SS. Mary & John still have very active congregations today.

INTERFAITH INTERFACE

Today it is not just Christianity that is followed on Cowley Road, as the area has become home to a more diverse community, with other religions also present. Muslims constitute one of the most important and active faith communities in East Oxford. When the first Muslims arrived in Oxford there was no mosque, so they used to say prayers in a restaurant along Walton Street. Eventually, in 1965, a mosque was purchased in Bath Street, which remains today. As the community increased, there was a pressing need for more mosques, and others were established in the area. One was established in Stanley Road, (a residential street between Iffley and Cowley Roads) in 1980, and another, the Bangladesh Mosque on Cowley Road opposite the Moonlight Restaurant in 1996. Different currents within Islam worship at different mosques.

Negotiating for a purpose-built mosque on Cowley Road has been a long process, but today there is finally a magnificent new building on the old Cowley Road Hospital site, which is set to be fully functional in 2005. This is known as the Central Mosque and has cost at least £1.5 million to build, funded by private donations from Muslims in the community.

Some progressive steps have been taken within the religious communities along Cowley Road. A Walk of Peace at the 2004 Carnival (see below) united Christians and Muslims during the potentially divisive period of the Iraq War. The walk was led by leaders of the Christian and Muslim communities and was given a high profile. Subsequently interfaith meetings, including the Jewish community, have been held, and there is ongoing liaison between different religious groups. Alwyn Samuel is a Christian priest who has been employed since 2003 to coordinate relations between the faiths. Overall, it is estimated that ten per cent of the community adhere to faiths other than Christianity, but there are relatively few Hindus or Sikhs in the area. Building up links between the faiths has been a continuing aim for several years, but since 9/11 has been more important. In December 2004 an Eid party organized by Sabir Hussain Mirza, a city councillor, was held at Oxford School and over 300 people from different faiths attended.

COWLEY ROAD CARNIVAL

Since 2001 the annual Cowley Road Carnival has been a growing success and has now become a multi-cultural celebration in the road. In 2004 approximately 20,000 people came to the colourful event, which is usually held in mid-June. Carnival history goes back to the mid-1980s when a group called Caribbean Focus, (a City Council initiative) was established, and from 1987 it was responsible for carnival celebrations in the city. Geno Humphrey, one of those involved at the time, remains active today and recalls how the lively processions consisted of floats with steel bands, discos and children dressed up, accompanied by people walking alongside them. At this stage the processions started and finished at different venues; for instance, one started at St. Giles and finished at South Park, while another started at Cowley Road and finished at Hinksey Park. There was a lapse in carnival continuity for a few years until it was picked up in 2001 by East Oxford Action, (EOA), a community action group, described in more detail in Chapter 5. EOA received a government grant to help improve the area, and one of the projects undertaken was the revival of the Cowley Road Carnival.

The Carnival has focused on bringing together different communities in the area with cultural activities, mainly concentrated in Manzil Way (the site of the old Cowley Road Hospital). The first Carnival witnessed the decoration of the building between the public conveniences and the Libra Project with multi-coloured handprints. This artwork can still be seen today and is a significant landmark on Cowley Road. There was music from rock bands, African percussion, Indian dance and samba throughout the day.

Over 15,000 people came to the second Carnival the following year, where 300 people, among them schoolchildren, musicians and members of the community, joined in a rainbow-themed procession through Cowley Road, the Plain, Morrell Avenue and Union Street. By 2003 the Carnival procession was getting bigger and more popular, and a multi-cultural procession included Chinese dragons, Punjabi dancers, Zimbabwean singers, samba dancers and schoolchildren. A new addition was a Carnival Queen, Councillor Olive Steadman from Littlemore.

Carnival was now becoming more than just a celebration for the residents of East Oxford, as people came from all over the city and beyond for the occasion. In response to requests, Cowley Road was closed for the Carnival in 2004, 2005 and 2007. It has now become a celebrated event that incorporates many aspects of the community. The *Oxford Mail* reported the event on 14 June 2004:

Carnival fever hit Cowley Road yesterday (June 13) as revellers scaled rooftops, fences and even a telephone box to catch a glimpse of the festival procession.

The fourth Cowley Road Carnival attracted about 16,000 people—with visitors packing the street to watch a colourful parade of about 1,000 people, led by a giant 18ft by 20ft mermaid.

This year's carnival had a much stronger Afro-Caribbean flavour than before, with a stage in Bullingdon Road where some of Oxford's biggest reggae, hip-hop and soul acts performed.

Tina Kuedrue, from Chesterfield, was visiting her sister in Headington, Oxford, and decided to come to the carnival. She said: "It is brilliant. I think it shows the different cultures you have here. I didn't realise there were so many different communities here and they all bring something to the carnival."

Laura Didcott, a teacher at Cutteslowe Primary School in Wren Road, north Oxford, said: "I had a lovely time. It was good to see so many kids there and there were lots of different nationalities around too. I might try and get my students involved in the procession next year!"

The Carnival has been described as "Cowley Road at its finest", and it is certainly a visual celebration of its mixture of cultures and a showcase for all the positive aspects of the area. Henrietta Gill the Carnival coordinator considers that local people feel very proud of Cowley Road and that the carnival is a celebration of this pride and passion. Each year has brought more integration from different community groups and now the Carnival has a range of sponsors such as Oxford Swindon & Gloucester Cooperative Society, The Arts Council of England and Oxford City Council. Carnival has grown into a splendid event that contributes to the promotion of Cowley Road.

CRIME AND PUNISHMENT

Cowley Road sometimes receives a less positive sort of press coverage, especially when the issue of street crime is raised.

Crime in East Oxford during the 1950s did not seem to present too much of a challenge for the local constabulary and was probably representative of the national picture. During the first three post-war decades nothing remarkable was reported in the area. Most trouble, although inconvenient and unpleasant for those involved, was low-key. Even so, some of these incidents were considered quite shocking by some. Just after Christmas in 1950, for instance the *Oxford Mail* published a piece on damage to property by hooligans in the area. It was reported that a gang of youths were operating after dark and damaging gates and gardens in East Oxford. In the wake of this vandalism, a local councillor asked the Council meeting in January to request the chief constable to investigate possibilities of special constables patrolling the area.

In April 1956 there was some trouble at the local cinema, the Regal, involving a gang of youths. This was at the height of the Teddy Boy era, a period which witnessed the beginnings of teenage culture involving other groups such as Beatniks. Teddy Boys were youths mainly from working-class backgrounds who wore distinctive clothes and had a reputation for violence. The report by the local newspaper tells of how the gang appeared threatening, as the management refused some 200 Teddy Boys admission to the cinema. The youths, who came from all over the city, then hung around the cinema and outside the University and City Arms, which resulted in the police being involved and requesting them to move on. An altercation occurred and a youth assaulted a policeman. He was later found guilty of this offence in court and fined. The newspaper helpfully described what the youth was wearing: a light-coloured drape jacket, dark trousers, pink socks and brown leather slip-on shoes—the standard uniform of Teddy Boys.

Other crimes in the 1950s included assaults, while a summons was issued against a local man for aiding and abetting the selling of ten eggs of the Moustached Warbler, contrary to the Protection of Birds Act 1954, but this charge was later dismissed. There was an incident involving a lorry and two cyclists riding abreast. The magistrates criticized this practice, apparently common among workers at the Cowley Works, reprimanding them for creating a road hazard. A shop owner was found guilty of three offences under the Food and Drugs Act 1955 and fined £50 for selling sweets (8oz Liquorice Allsorts) that were unfit to eat.

During the late 1950s and early 1960s crime nationally was said to be on the increase and this was noted at a local level following a spate of break-ins. "Smash and grabs" were robberies, usually in shops, when the glass window was smashed and goods quickly snatched. As the goods had to have some street market value, shops selling electrical goods were particularly targeted. There were several in Cowley Road, and in the 1950s this form of robbery generated sensationalist local press coverage. Six cameras worth £150 were stolen from a smash and grab raid from Robert Stanley at 212 Cowley Road. "A brick was thrown through the plate glass window and the thief in grabbing the cameras swept the rest of the display aside." The alarm was raised by a passer-by who had seen two men running from the shop and telephoned the police who searched the area without success. Meanwhile, a German woman visitor was robbed of £45 in one of three burglaries in East Oxford one Saturday night. The Chief Constable stated in the *Oxford Times* that he thought this was typical of the increase in crime all over the country.

Smash and grabs continued in the early 1970s, but another form of robbery, known as "muggings", swept the country at the same time. Mugging victims were usually portrayed as elderly woman who would have their handbags snatched by youths. In reality, muggers were more likely to be anybody and would "mug" anybody who looked as if they had something worthwhile to steal. At one stage East Oxford was considered a "mugger's paradise", according to a local councillor following three muggings in the area.

Although there have been murders in the area, these have usually been "domestic" in nature. There was a particular nasty period for women in the mid-1980s when a man known as the East Oxford rapist was terrorizing the area. He was eventually caught and sentenced. Drug-related crime is, of course, another symptom of changing populations, and East Oxford, like any inner-city area, has its fair share of such criminality. Efforts have been made by the police to counteract drug dealing, and most people consider that Cowley Road is much improved on this score. Nowadays there is also a more relaxed policy towards particular drugs such as cannabis, and this has had repercussions in the form of declining drug-related crime. Vandalism, however, continues to be the bane of many residents' lives as mindless louts damage anything from cars to gardens.

Over the last fifty years levels of crime locally have risen steeply. This increase can be partly attributed to the changing character of the area and also to national crime trends. The advent of supermarkets, for instance, has made shoplifting easier, while the introduction of credit cards has encouraged more fraud-related crimes. At the same time, increased car ownership has led to an increase in car crime. The widespread ownership of consumer items such as DVDs and computers has provided easy targets for burglars, especially those financing expensive drug habits. Other causes of increased crime rates have been attributed to the decline of the nuclear family, decline in moral standards and the lack of respect for authority, and greater use of alcohol and drugs. High unemployment levels and social exclusion are seen as other influences that have increased crime rates, a relevant factor in an area such as East Oxford which still has pockets of deprivation.

Policing has changed over the past half century. There is still some community relationship between police and public, but some law enforcement is influenced by government targets and policy and driven by performance indicators at a local level. Community policemen have spoken very positively about their role in the area. One resident who lived on Cowley Road in the 1970s recalls an interesting incident when driving up the street that captures a good-humoured policing response:

> We pass a policeman on a bike. Ray starts screaming OINK OINK OINK at him. We carry on. The inevitable happens. The traffic light is on red and as we wait we see the policeman cycling slowly up towards us. We're still stopped when he reaches us. He taps on the passenger window, which Ray reluctantly winds down. Policeman ignores him but in a very matter of fact tone asks John [the driver] if he has a licence to carry livestock.

Police now patrol on bikes, which is reminiscent of times gone by, and are reported to be a big success in the community. But their equipment has otherwise changed with time and health and safety regulations. Truncheons and handcuffs were essential items for police officers in the 1950s and 1960s, but these are largely a thing of the past, as the mobile phone has replaced the whistle and the police box.

There is occasionally sensational crime in East Oxford, but on the whole lawlessness is relatively unremarkable. The area is arguably less violent than the city centre, and a lot of crime is drug- or alcohol-related such as car vandalism and is concentrated in the streets off Cowley Road. Local policeman often state that they would rather police Cowley Road on a Friday or Saturday night than be in the city centre.

THE SEEDY SIDE

No inner-city street would be complete without a seedy side, and Cowley Road is no exception. Lap dancers at local bars and two sex shops are not what many residents want, and protests have been made. Just like any other business, the sex industry has capitalized on the lively popularity of Cowley Road, and prostitution is said to be on the increase in the area. The police insist that the area does not have a problem with prostitution in comparison with other cities and would act appropriately if they receive complaints. Residents voiced a different opinion to that of the police at the East Area Committee in August 2004, and claimed that the problem was serious, particularly in some side streets.

Another contentious problem is that of perpetual litter in the road. In April 2004 Cowley Road received a nomination as one of Britain's shabbiest streets by listeners in a Radio 5 Live survey. Although there are perpetual litter problems, due to some extent to a large number of take-away restaurants on a busy main road, some people were surprised that this should warrant such a nomination.

But Cowley Road has long had to contend with some of the worst sorts of urban problem, not least planning blight, as the next chapter reveals.

2

FOR THE GREATER GOOD: PLANNERS VERSUS PEOPLE

Even back in the 1920s, traffic management was already an issue in congested Oxford. A plan to redevelop the city's road system was put into action after the First World War, and schemes continued to be proposed thereafter. Underpinning all redevelopment plans, at least after 1945, were two major aims: to preserve the ancient university area, and to develop another Oxford east of the ancient city. Some of the plans affected other areas of the city, and in fact several plans were proposed to address traffic relief over a period of twenty or so years. This chapter looks at the history of these various schemes and shows how they affected the development of Cowley Road for over fifty years.

BIRTH OF OXFORD TRANSPORT STRATEGY

In 1923 the City Council had produced a town planning scheme in line with national developments and trends. A draft plan for an outer bypass was approved in 1927, and by 1935 the first section of the northern bypass was completed. During the war years the development was still being discussed; in December 1941 the City Council approved a report from the Town Planning Committee, recommending that the old part of the city should have a ring road around it, and that a new civic and business centre be established on the east side of Magdalen Bridge. This would mean that traffic would be diverted away from the city centre. Roland Newman describes the background, chronology and complexities of Oxford's traffic plans in detail in *The Road and Christ Church Meadow*. A road scheme subsequently emerged, involving an inner ring road that would run south of Christ Church Meadow and hence bypass the city centre.

Dr. Thomas Sharp was appointed by Oxford City Council as a consultant town planner in 1945, and was directed to produce a report on the planning and development of the city. His plan was published in 1948: *Oxford Replanned*. Among his 52 conclusions he believed that Oxford should remain one city, and he designed a new road across the northern edge of Christ Church Meadow (this road was to be known as Merton Mall) and over to St. Aldates with the road forking in two directions—one towards the railway station and the other northwards. Another of Sharp's recommendations was that the Cowley car factories should be relocated outside the city on the basis that there were "no geographical, social or economic reasons" for their then position.

Most of the debate around his plan was concentrated on the road across Christ Church Meadow. This debate posed a conflict: the need for traffic reduction in the city versus the sacrificing of an open space (Christ Church Meadow) in the middle of a city. There was subsequently much local and national discussion, and alternative plans were mooted. Many organizations took part in the discussions, including Oxford University, the Trades Council, the Chamber of Trade, the House of Lords and various prominent individuals and politicians. Even within these organizations there were conflicting opinions. The plan to create an inner ring road was a political hot potato, as it involved the desecration of the meadow and demolishing parts of the historic areas of the city.

It is evident that the inner relief road plans were both highly controversial and constantly changing, and it is also clear that the overall city redevelopment plans envisaged the creation of two Oxfords: the ancient city and a new town. Plans were initially made for municipal buildings to be established in East Oxford. The area was already a thriving shopping centre. But along the way another plan materialized in the 1950s—the development of Cowley Centre, known today as Templar's Square. Cowley and its surrounding areas such as Florence Park were expanding and a new estate, Blackbird Leys, was planned.

After the war some British cities had suffered bomb damage (luckily Oxford escaped this fate) and had to be reconstructed. In many areas a new development policy relocated parts of the population to new "green field" developments such as Blackbird Leys. Obviously Blackbird Leys needed shopping and other facilities. Although not directly related to the inner relief road, this plan was interlinked with the development and future of Cowley Road. In the 1950s, then, there were contentious plans for traffic relief in the city, plans for a new civic centre to be established in East Oxford and a plan to create a new shopping centre in Cowley.

During the 1950s debates over the route of the inner relief road contained various proposals, most of which would have affected Cowley Road in one way or another. These plans naturally created controversy but at the same time, some proposed alterations to property in Cowley Road were rejected if they interfered with the overall development plan. One curious example is to be found in an article in the *Oxford Times* of 6 July 1951, when academic nutrition expert Dr. Hugh McDonald Sinclair, the owner of 35 Cowley Road, then a greengrocer's shop, applied to the City Council for permission to alter the property. Dr. Sinclair's intention was to continue to expand the business and to house a manager in a flat above the shop. As the premises had no bedrooms and the kitchen and sanitary arrangements were "somewhat rudimentary", he wanted to modernize the property. Bizarrely, the Council agreed to an application for an extension, but on condition that the extra building should be removed and the ground cleared by 3 December 1965.

It seems that Dr. Sinclair was caught up in development plans for Cowley Road. In the light of the proposed municipal buildings it was necessary for the Council to make provisos on planning applications. Alterations to the shop front had been allowed, yet the alterations at the back, away from the road, were, it seems, likely to be only temporary and subject to a future demolition order, leaving the owner at a loss to understand the apparent inconsistency. An architect representing the owner at an appeal said that the alterations to the shop front made the proposed extensions at the back the next step. "It would be a shockingly wasteful step to pull down the proposed improvements in fifteen years," he concluded.

Representatives of the City Council informed the appeal hearing of the reasons for the decision in relation to Cowley Road's redevelopment. Mr. Astley, assistant solicitor to the City Council, stressed the importance of the area and stated that the "Cowley Road area is of first importance to the re-development of Oxford." His colleague, Mr. Mason, the chief town planning assistant, spoke of the traffic problem in Cowley Road, saying that this alone made redevelopment essential. He went on to justify the reasons for the rede-velopment of the Cowley Road district and the need to find additional space for public buildings for a new town hall, public health buildings, a museum and libraries. Cowley Road, it seems, was earmarked to be the geographical centre of a new town. Improvements to existing property in the area were seen by the Council as delaying the time when full-scale redevelopment could begin.

More suggestions that Cowley Road was to be directly affected by the overall city redevelopment emerged at the first public inquiry regarding the road scheme proposals in March 1953. A Council spokesperson, reported the *Oxford Times*, announced that the redevelopment of "that part of the city" was to be considered by the Council later and that "it will become necessary to improve traffic conditions in St. Clements, Cowley Road and the Plain junction." Furthermore, it was announced that a site was reserved for public buildings at the Plain itself and in the westerly part of St. Clements for the university. It was the Council's intention to see that the eastern approach to Magdalen Bridge was improved in its appearance and made "more fitting as a gateway to the ancient city."

The embargo on development on Cowley Road was more explicit in 1959. An *Oxford Times* headline stated: "Ban on Cowley Road Development—City Council Will Protect Shopping Centre". The article continued:

Further shopping development along parts of the Cowley Road will be opposed by Oxford City Council Planning Committee. This was revealed yesterday by Mr Chandler, City Architect, following refusal of the Ministry of Housing to allow a new shop to be opened on the Cowley Road, because "it would increase traffic congestion and might reduce the effectiveness of the new shopping centre at Cowley."

The Minister's decision was welcomed by Alderman P D Brown, chair of Planning Committee: "it is quite true that more shops in Cowley Road would do what the Minister says. We want to encourage traders to the Cowley Centre and it is welcome news that the Minister backs us up and the sort of thing one expects him to do. Mr Chandler... said of the minister's decision: "that is exactly what we feel. It is very encouraging that we should adopt the same view." Mr Chandler said yesterday: "It is firm policy to limit shopping development on Cowley Road in the area from Princes Street to Cowley Road Hospital and for a similar area on the other side. We don't think there should be any additional development in those areas."

A Ministry official visited the site according to "accompanied visit procedure" which rules out the necessity for a public enquiry. In his report, says the minister, the officer "notes that in the immediate neighbourhood of the appeal premises there are a number of shops and other uses interspersed between residential properties, but that the Cowley Road becomes increasingly residential in character to the south east of Divinity Road and Leopold Street."

This extract gives an insight into just how the embargo was taking effect in the community. Oxford City Council was strongly in support of the Cowley Centre development, but was this to the detriment of Cowley Road? Development at this time could have been crucial for the future of the road. There were old buildings in need of modernization, as seen in the case of no. 35. The City Council recognized that there was potential for commercial development on Cowley Road but did not want to deter trade from the new Cowley Centre. Now, probably by default, the Cowley Centre development had become intrinsically linked with Cowley Road's future.

Despite the ban on developing the area, some attempt was made to improve Cowley Road in 1959. Oxford Trades Council had originally drawn attention to the dilapidated seats in front of Cowley Road Hospital in 1951. This area was eventually turned into a garden, so that older people who were patients in the hospital could sit outside.

Cowley Centre development plans also courted controversy. One opponent of this development was the eminent Lord Beveridge, one time Master of University College and architect of the welfare state reforms, who spoke of "rescuing Oxford". At the end of 1957 he spoke publicly about his views, which were reported in the *Oxford Times*. He linked his opposition to the need to relieve traffic congestion in the city and maintained that the new shopping centre was in the wrong place to achieve this aim. His alternative proposal was that a shopping centre should be located in East Oxford near the Plain. He dreamed of borrowing £1m from Lord Nuffield to establish a new town centre in East Oxford and was of the opinion that any such investment would immediately pay for itself as the majority of the then population of Oxford (70,000 out of 114,000) lived east of the Cherwell.

Lord Beveridge considered that the "solution of the problem is not by-passes... nor is there any solution in making any more roads... The only solution is to make a real centre east of Magdalen Bridge with entertainments, offices and everything. Will a centre in Cowley really solve the problem? Not at all because it is no good in itself, but because it is ultimately in the wrong place altogether." He was concerned that Oxford, like everywhere else, would grow indefinitely by adding suburbs around the centre.

Over the course of several decades, due to successful lobbying and Government Inquiry decisions, a variety of plans were submitted which involved demolishing homes and businesses in parts of the city; and of course being caught up in the Cowley Centre development complicated matters further. One such plan was for a route along Bullingdon Road and Jackdaw

Lane. Another proposed route was through Dawson Street and Cowley Road.

THE INNER RELIEF ROAD

One of the major issues facing East Oxford residents in the 1950s was the potential threat of the relief roads cutting through their community. As we have seen, discussion on the proposals and counter-proposals for the relief roads was in the main carried out within institutions and organizations such as the university, political parties and trade unions. Yet the ultimate decisions were taken by Oxford City Council, and at this time there was a strong and influential university presence on this body. At the beginning of 1956, 26 out of 68 Council members objected to the proposals for the inner relief road scheme which would have included streets in Central and North Oxford and Christ Church Meadow. Opposition to different parts of the plan came from a variety of organizations, and the overall reaction to the plan as a whole was complex as it involved different parts of the city. The university was a key player in the opposition movement, and a detailed account of the resistance to the plan can be found in *The Road and Christ Church Meadow*. (The information in this section has been compiled from Dr. Newman's study, extracts from the *Oxford Times* and *East Oxford Advertiser*, local radio interviews and residents' memories.)

When the first plan was presented in the 1950s, the major objections were voiced by established institutions. With regard to those representing local residents and businesses in Cowley Road, it was principally the East Ward Labour Party that articulated opposition. It objected to the initial total plan, set up a sub-committee and arranged a public meeting to discover local residents' opinions.

The results of the first Inquiry into the relief road plans were published in September 1956. The Minister of Housing and Local Government, Duncan Sandys, stated that the Public Inquiry in February showed that the Council's road scheme had "altogether failed to reconcile conflicting opinions." Consequently he had rejected both the plans presented at this time. He requested that the Council design new proposals for an inner bypass across the northern part of Christ Church Meadow as that would relieve the High Street of traffic, link the east to the rest of the city and close Magdalen Bridge to traffic.

The Inquiry held in 1960 considered three basic themes for the road: Scheme A, a relief road that went across the south of the Meadow; Scheme B, a road across the northern edge of the Meadow and the closure of Magdalen Bridge; and Scheme C, a road across the central Meadow and the closure of Magdalen Bridge. The Council's proposal was a mix of A and B. All sorts of objections were made to these proposals and mainly revolved around the different colleges' interests. Sir Frederick Amer, the Inspector, recommended that the Council's scheme should be adopted—a road across the Meadow. A plan for a sunken road across the Meadow was then submitted to the Council as part of the Development Plan in September 1963, which was approved. In the meantime, in November 1963, the Buchanan Report, *Traffic in Towns*, brought about a national change in transport planning policy by acknowledging the need for towns to adapt to accommodate the increase in traffic.

This latest plan presented more concern for the residents of Cowley Road. In order for an inner relief road along the lines recommended by the Inspector to be built, the City Council would have to demolish homes and buildings in the area. Although not in the direct path of the proposed route, one of the affected streets was Alma Place, a cul-de-sac off Cowley Road. Many of these homes were designated for compulsory purchase. The residents were understandably angry with the Council for obvious reasons, as many had spent considerable sums of money on improving their Victorian homes. One resident had moved in two and half years previously, purchased the house on a Council mortgage and was assured that Alma Place would not be affected by development.

A Save Alma Place group was formed, and a surveyor and solicitor were employed to represent residents in the next Inquiry on a relief road in 1965. An alternative scheme that would make the demolition of their houses unnecessary was proposed. The *Oxford Times* ran a piece entitled "Second Battle of Alma: Residents to Fight Compulsory Purchase." The article revealed that residents were prepared to stand up to the plans, had become more organized and wanted to defend their homes and community from redevelopment. There were 122 objections to the plan at the Inquiry, coming from organizations and individuals in Alma Place, Jeune Street, Stockmore Street, Magdalen Road, Boulter Street and Cowley Road. Many of these had homes or businesses that were designated for compulsory purchase.

In January 1966 the Minister of Housing and Local Government, Richard Crossman, announced the decision to stop the Meadow road. Oxford City Council appointed consultants to examine new possible routes for a relief road and announced the plans in December 1968. This new route was described in the *Oxford Times*. It was to run from Abingdon Road, north of

Eastwyke Farm, through the university rugby ground, across Iffley Road; it then passed through Bullingdon Road, curved from the College of Further Education under Cowley Road to Organs builders yard, then under Morrell Avenue and the western end of South Park to join Headington Hill. The total cost was to be £31m, and the Council was urged to avoid delay and start the plan in 1973.

This scheme was clearly an alternative to the earlier plan to site a road through Christ Church Meadow. The university had been successful in its opposition to the Meadow project, and as a result a central part of East Oxford and parts of South Oxford were to be demolished instead. Needless to say, this latest plan was extremely contentious as the road was to run through residential areas, destroying homes, businesses and communities.

Residents heard about this dramatic plan from their local newspaper and were understandably shocked. Pat Clements described to me how she heard of the scheme:

> I first heard about the road proposals from the *Oxford Mail* in 1968. No one was "told", it was just announced in the paper as far as I am aware. Following that announcement everyone was up in arms, so I assume we all found out in the same way. At that time there was still something of a community in the area, people had lived there for years and knew their neighbours. I felt that would be destroyed. Several of those to be affected were elderly and would lose lifelong friends and possibly not withstand the stress and strain of losing their home. Many were really distressed at the prospect.

Mrs. Clements was not alone in receiving the news in this way. John Purves also recalls how he heard the news that the proposed road would be cutting through his community: "I heard [the news by] the usual Council technique—I discovered the plans via the press just before a national holiday [Christmas]."

After digesting the rather shocking news, Mrs. Clements got to work very quickly with a neighbour, Joan Parchment, and organized a public meeting in early January at Cowley St. John School. Over 200 residents from East and South Oxford attended this meeting, and the "View or You Campaign" group was formed. Mrs. Clements and Mrs. Parchment had been told by Council officials that 169 houses and 42 businesses would be involved. This would, of course, have had a tremendous impact on East Oxford.

Two Labour councillors, Olive Gibbs and Roger Dudman, attended the meeting, reported the *Oxford Times*, and supported the campaign. Olive Gibbs said that "the reason for this road is to preserve that swampy filthy piece of Christ Church Meadow which nobody walks through as far as I can see except poets or people contemplating suicide." (While this statement might sound incongruous today, to be fair to Olive Gibbs, people have commented on how Christ Church Meadow was in a different state in those days.) Councillor Gibbs also pointed out that it would be difficult to re-house families displaced through compulsory purchase orders as the housing problem in the city was already chronic. Strong feelings against the university were also heard; Mr. Parchment, a resident from Bullingdon Road, asked the question, "Are we a satellite revolving around the university?" and was applauded by the meeting.

An active campaign, led by local people who were to be severely affected by this plan, swung into action. They called for meetings with the local MP, leafleted, organized public meetings and press campaigns, and sent a petition to Downing Street. (In fact, two rival petitions circulated in East Oxford, one in favour of the road, one against, although the latter movement was short-lived.) In East Oxford the following streets were to be affected: Cowley Road, Hurst Street, St. Mary's Road, Bullingdon Road, Iffley Road, Union Street, Chapel Street and Morrell Avenue. Another public meeting held in the town hall in February was unanimous in believing that the relief road would destroy East Oxford.

Council officers attended meetings in order to provide information and allay fears. Mrs. Clements suggests that these officials merely tolerated the campaign leaders, who were permanently asking questions, and found them a "thorn in their side". Housing areas, meanwhile, were reserved for those who would be hit by the relief road. The city architect informed a meeting that families from East and South Oxford whose homes were to be demolished would be re-housed at Donnington and Grandpont. A stormy meeting at Oxford School was told that part of the Donnington allotments and the old gas works site had been set aside for housing. But it was also made clear that no businesses were envisaged on these sites; they would simply have to go elsewhere. At this time there were apparently already 2,000 people waiting for homes in the city. The extra families made homeless by the road scheme would have added much more pressure onto an already overstretched resource.

Oxford Trades Council believed that the plan was the result of the university having ultimate power at the expense of local residents. Although some local politicians were opposed to the plan, the Council as a whole was not, and a motion to delay the decision on the road was defeated in a Council meeting in March 1969. In general, residents thought that the Liberals were the only political party against the scheme. After examining consultants' reports, the coordinating committee urged the Council to adopt the Eastwyke Farm scheme, and claimed that it would reduce traffic at key points in the city and offer greater opportunities to improve the environment of East Oxford. Proposals included a pedestrian precinct in Cowley Road from Chapel Street to James Street and traffic restrictions (except for buses). Interestingly, in light of the issue of blocked planning permissions, the Council also announced that once the road network had been settled, homes would be brought up to standard in East Oxford. It also seems that a possible improvement and rehabilitation programme for the area had been dropped by the Council in 1965 in favour of Jericho because of the delay caused by the road issue. Overall, the Council maintained that these plans, along with the removal of an industrialized area near Union Street and East Avenue, would improve conditions in East Oxford.

At the Council meeting in April a poignant speech was made by Alderman Lionel Harrison (Conservative) as he outlined the situation faced

by people in East Oxford. The area, he said, "has suffered from 'planning blight' for the past twenty years. It is rapidly becoming the poorest and worst area of the whole city. The area around the Plain is gradually decaying because of the uncertainty of where the road is going." There was no doubt within the community, he remarked, that the strength of feeling against the road was strong. Another Conservative member, Ben Tannant, spoke against the road: "It would cause chaos if we agree to the Eastwyke Farm route… it would finish East Oxford as a community."

Also raised at this meeting was the effect that the reorganization of the city's education system was having on local children. A decision had been made to reorganize the schools from a two-tier to a three-tier system some years previously, and finding a suitable school site in the middle of the planning blight was another consequence of the inner relief road saga, which meant that children were being educated in unsatisfactory conditions in temporary buildings. Yet despite these objections and local action, the revised road plan for the city was approved by the Council and scheduled to start in 1972. It was envisaged that the project would be completed in 1991, 19 years later.

Opposition to the road continued, and Mrs. Clements and Mrs. Parchment walked to Downing Street to deliver a petition. Mrs. Clements did this because she wanted to generate more interest in the matter across the city:

> Joan and I decided we would walk to London to get publicity. It was mainly those who were likely to be involved who were aware of what was proposed and we wanted to let the whole city know. We took up a petition and that went with us and was delivered to No.10. At that time you could still walk right up to the door and knock.

It took two and half days to walk to London. The Liberals were very supportive, following in a car and providing food and first aid. Mrs. Parchment remembers getting a lot of blisters and Mrs Clements recalls:

> It took us two whole days (we stopped at night for safety reasons) and the people were incredibly supportive. Some acted as marshals and checked up on us from time to time by car. Others paid our overnight expenses. I can remember one man, he was the Liberal agent at the time, took off my shoes by the roadside and tended to my blisters! When we arrived at Downing Street it was not shut off like it is now and there was a huge crowd of people around the door area. We just thought it was a demo until

we got nearer and then my two children ran up to greet us. They were all supporters who had hired a coach to come and cheer us to the door. We knocked on the door and handed in the petition. The downside was that my son, when he grinned at me, had no front teeth. He had been knocked down by a car on Cowley Road.

Evan Luard, the local Labour MP, met with the East Oxford Residents' Association (EORA) and conveyed their opposition to the Minister of Housing, thus reinforcing the message of the petition. Mrs. Clements and her colleagues certainly went all out to campaign against the scheme and received a lot of community support. She says: "All those under threat of losing their homes were very supportive, others gradually became aware of what was proposed and were supportive. We didn't know if it would happen, but were frightened by the determination of the City Council. However, we were determined to try to prevent it at all costs."

THE 1970 INQUIRY

Yet another Inquiry was conducted in November 1970 (the third in ten years). It heard evidence from local residents on how their lives and communities were being affected by the proposed road route. Residents hired counsel, which was costly, but the funds were raised by collections at meetings, a sweepstake and requests for donations. People were very generous, according to Mrs Clements.

For one opponent of the scheme who gave evidence at the Inquiry, the situation was very clear: the demolition of 400 homes was simply a sacrifice in order to save Christ Church Meadow. EORA also voiced a strong objection to the road on the grounds that the loss of housing would be severe and the effects on the environment considerable. EORA also made the following very pertinent points: that the mixture of home ownership and rented properties in the area at relatively low prices was an asset which should be maintained; that the disruptive process of road building—noise, dirt, smell and visual intrusion—would cause a loss of confidence in the area; that the road would cut the area in two and would have a damaging impact on a residential area where community ties were strong; that little information was given to immigrants who could not understand English. Furthermore, EORA argued, most of the residents of the area could not afford to buy their way out of the path of the impending nuisance, and the organization called for a policy of participation and partnership between residents and the City Council.

COWLEY ROAD

As the plans unfolded and became clearer, it was apparent that a secondary road was going to be necessary to develop a link between Cowley and Iffley Roads and Headington Hill. Marston Street was the only existing direct road that could serve this purpose and was hence under consideration for massive enlargement. A letter of protest from the Society of St. John the Evangelist, or the Cowley Fathers, in Marston Street was submitted to the Inquiry. The Cowley Fathers argued that "the increase of traffic would injure our work, more particularly as the buildings are used as a house of retreat and quiet for many people who come here for a time of rest and meditation." Other inadequate procedures were also identified. One of the consultants admitted to the Inquiry that residents of Cowley Road had not been consulted individually when consultants were preparing their plan for a "pedestrian segregated" area in Cowley Road between its junction with Bullingdon Road and Marston Street.

Although there were a number of options on the table for the Inquiry to decide upon, for people in East Oxford the issue was plain. The abandonment of the Christ Church Meadow plan, first designed by Thomas Sharp, meant the implementation of Eastwyke Farm plan, which was destined to cut through Cowley Road and demolish homes and businesses in the area. Mr. W.J. Glover, QC for the City Council, denied that the Council had gone back on it word: "One regrets the demolition of these houses, one regrets the uncertainty, but this demolition is necessary to solve the accepted Oxford traffic problem." He put this question to the Inquiry: "Is the damage to East Oxford such that an otherwise proper solution to Oxford's traffic problems cannot be adopted?" He was probably voicing the opinion of many in the city outside East Oxford, suggesting that Oxford as a whole would benefit from the new scheme, even if Cowley Road had to be sacrificed.

BEYOND THE INQUIRY

The "View or You" campaign seemed to have triumphed when the Inspector finally decided in favour of the sunken road through Christ Church Meadow. But in October 1971, the Secretary of State, Peter Walker, overruled the Inquiry's conclusion and opted for the Eastwyke Farm route. This move rejuvenated the campaign, as residents were stunned that the Minister had not accepted the findings of the Inquiry. "What price democracy and justice?" asked one resident. People in the community "had believed in the normal process and channels of democracy—a fair hearing leading to a fair verdict—but this was not like that." The outcome was a "disillusionment that continued in the area," and according to one resident, many thought that the political representatives had "told lies". Following the news of Walker's ruling, nearly 300 residents attended a public meeting and were urged by two Labour Party councillors to fight on. The City Council, meanwhile, accepted the Minister's recommendation, regardless of protests from Labour members.

Oxford City Labour Party subsequently revised its transport policy. Local Liberals sought the advice of Ralph Nader, who was had made his name as an environmentalist in the United States and now a leading Green politician. A working party was established in June 1972. It had a brief to review the transportation problem of Oxford without resorting to major road construction, on the premise that a balanced provision would achieve a better environment for the whole of the city by reducing the number of vehicles using the city's roads. This was the beginning of the city's balanced transport policy.

Another knock-on effect of the uncertainty affecting the neighbourhood was the postponement in the building of the awaited East Oxford Middle School, since no site had yet been decided upon because of the road proposals. The Council wrote to Peter Walker, requesting him to reconsider the decision not to allow the building of school on the university rugby ground on Iffley Road. When, in December 1971, the Council gave the go-ahead for the relief road, the Meadow Lane site was approved for the middle school. Objections to the new school site were received, and early in 1972 the planning committee deferred the decision for two weeks for the Minister to assess the issues involved. Meanwhile, parents were becoming concerned about their children's education. An action committee had been formed, and activists threatened to occupy the Chief Education Officer's office in an attempt to have their children's education discussed.

The proposed middle school site was also a highly sensitive affair. Some of the objections to the site were tied in with objections to the Eastwyke Farm road and others were based on conservation criteria. Eventually the City Council approved the site by 28 to 25 in March 1972 despite petitions from the East Oxford Protection and Improvement Society, the Liberals and Iffley Road Traders.

In May 1972 local elections shifted the balance of power on the City Council in Labour's favour and the Labour-dominated Council abandoned the Eastwyke Farm Road plan. Tom Blundell, the committee chairman, remarked that "this decision will be seen by present and future generations of Oxford students, dons, environmentalists, conservationists and even a few conservatives as a unique contribution to the preservation of the Oxford we all love."

But even then, the debate did not stop, as in September Environment Secretary Peter Walker informed the City Council that the inner relief road must be kept in the Oxford Development Plan and that the road could become a possibility in the future. (Local authorities were required under the 1947 Town and Country Planning Act to produce a Development Plan for Ministerial approval.) This meant that property in the line of the route would continue to be blighted. EORA launched a mass campaign to fight Walker's decision, highlighting the planning blight problem and long-term planning implications for the community.

Further complications arose following elections in May 1974 when the newly established Oxfordshire County Council took over major planning decisions on highways. This council was controlled by the Conservative Party, and it announced that intended to resurrect the inner relief road and even devised new plans which cut costs and involved less demolition, but there was conflict between Conservatives representing rural areas and some of those representing urban areas. For people living outside the city the urban relief road was an attractive scheme, as in theory it would make journeys easier; for those directly affected, it was an altogether different matter and some city Conservatives were aware of this. Not all city Conservatives, however, were of this opinion; Lady Young, a senior Conservative City Councillor, was one of the main supporters of the inner road plans.

Oxford City Council, meanwhile, decided to complain to the Secretary of State in 1975 that the County Council transport plans were holding up developments in the city, particularly with regard to housing. As the issue again seemed to threaten Cowley Road's future, protests escalated, and in November 1975 several groups such as Shelter and Oxford Housing Action Group joined forces with residents to campaign against the road. Local politicians also submitted objections to the County Council's proposals.

Finally, in August 1978, Peter Shore, the Secretary of State for the Environment, announced his decision to delete all references in the local plan to an inner relief road, including the controversial Eastwyke Farm route. This decision angered Conservative leaders, who remained in favour of the relief road scheme and planned to oppose Shore's ruling, but ultimately the road plan died because of political and economic problems in central government. Hit by a balance-of-payments crisis, Labour Prime Minister James Callaghan had been forced to borrow money from the International Monetary Fund (IMF), and a condition of this loan was that there was to be a curb on public spending. As a result, from the mid-1970s local authorities had to reduce their budgets, and Oxfordshire County Council was no exception. Services and investment of all sorts were cut, including road projects. Further plans for the inner relief road seemed to fade away after the advent of the IMF's austerity programme.

RESIDENTS' UPRISING

Around June 1972 a working party established by the City Council had produced a report on a local plan for East Oxford. After consultation with residents, this plan included schemes for road closures and traffic management, improved services, a rethink of the middle school site, limited shops on Cowley Road and a pedestrian area. Some of these ideas had been initiated by residents themselves and were not solely notions created by the Council.

Various community and action groups had become established by this time. These were: East Oxford Residents' Association, (formed in 1968), Schools Action Committee, East Oxford Neighbourhood House, (a new community project funded by an Urban Aid Grant) and *East Oxford Advertiser* (EOA), a community newspaper (started in 1970). More details about these organizations are in Chapter 5. There were also the beginnings of a community association. While each group had a different perspective, all were working to improve the community. The EOA was a successful medium of communication for residents, while the residents' association also had a newspaper that kept the community informed. Plans drawn up by the residents for East Oxford included a central complex for the middle school, a health centre and community centre, a library, a swimming pool and car park. As well as these facilities the residents wanted many residential streets closed to traffic and a pedestrian precinct in Cowley Road. New businesses would be discouraged, and acceptable local industry transferred to an industrial zone east of Boulter Street. The residents wanted land to be released for play schemes, garages and council houses and suggested that the best site for the middle school was Tuckwells (behind Tesco) or Oriel College sports ground. There was a call for a general improvement programme with attention to houses, trees, security areas, lights, pavements, lavatories, control of dogs and steps to be taken to deal with vagrants.

Residents involved in these activities were at that point meeting at 151a Cowley Road, the site of the present-day Boots (long-standing residents remember this as a children's clinic). Many other localities in Oxford, such as Cowley, Rose Hill and Donnington, had already established community centres but the Cowley Road area was without. By September the plan that went to Council incorporated a recommendation that it should buy property for community use, namely the Cowley St. John School (this was later to become East Oxford Community Centre). There was to be a further study on traffic and housing in the area and a series of public meetings on the local plan.

It is easy to see how and why local residents became active in local politics, as so many aspects of their lives were affected by Council decisions, some determined by central government and others not. Of course, the inner relief road scheme had had a severe impact on the stability of the area, with impending demolition, planning blight and lack of business and residential improvements influential in shaping its character. For many, the way that the Council had behaved over the road plan was a "political awakening", and the campaign was a popular success because, according to one resident, "it mobilized people who thought they were not going to be pushed around." Added to this was the knock-on effect the instability had on other services such as the delay in building a much-needed middle school.

It is no wonder, then, that local residents became involved in community action in East Oxford. The following letter from Neville Fowler, chairman of the East Oxford Residents' Association, published in the *Oxford Times* in 1972, illustrates how the road scheme the question of the new school and general problems in the area were all interlinked, and how political the situation was:

> It becomes increasingly difficult to take Lady Young seriously—surely a great handicap for anyone in public life. Her latest assertion that "a lot of people in east Oxford don't want a new middle school" is a hilarious example. By what peculiar logic or through what strange evidence does she arrive at this fantastic conclusion?
>
> Presumably to her distorted perception the fact that we peasants of east Oxford dared to ignore her veiled threats and opposed her party's cherished scheme to build our school in the river plain is sufficient proof of her anti-educational sentiments. The fact that we asked for a better site where the school could be more integrated into the community it is to serve apparently does not influence her assessment.
>
> The saga of the middle school site teaches a lesson that so far as the present majority on the city council are concerned, ordinary people and their needs come right at the bottom of the list of priorities and in order to maintain that situation they are prepared to stop their ears entirely to the voice of their electorate.

In an area like east Oxford we see this philosophy being applied every day. Council property is sold and homes pulled down to make way for university extensions. Immediately adjacent to our overcrowded school playground we see more council property turned into a car park which will chiefly benefit adjoining supermarkets. Other homes are to be destroyed to permit the construction of a crazy urban motorway, not to mention the desecration of our one remaining open space South Park.

Still more council owned property which is suitable for community use is to be demolished and replaced by profitable shops and offices. We dread to imagine the fate of the Cowley Road Hospital site when the hospital authorities vacate it late this decade. Will that too be hived off for some anti-social but profitable purpose?

This trend has to be halted and then reversed. The residents of this area will not stand idly by and witness a continuance of this university and commercial carve-up. We want to live in east Oxford.

Further letters followed, emphasizing that many residents felt that that only token consultations had taken place with regard to the new plans for East Oxford. While residents had been active in drawing up plans for their community, which were fed to the Council, they were of the opinion that they were not being taken seriously. The response from residents in Alma Place in the 1960s had shown the beginning of organized protest. A growing level of community activism in the early 1970s can perhaps be attributed to the more radical political climate of the time, as people were certainly becoming more assertive, as well as to the personalities of the residents themselves. In any case, there is no doubt that the overall development plan was a catalyst for local organization and provided the springboard for future community politics.

It is finally worth asking whether the road would have ever actually have been built, as it was such a massively controversial project that created enormous divisions in the city. Some people and politicians may well have held the view that the road, particularly the Christ Church Meadow route, was never going to materialize, especially as the university had an overwhelming influence in local and national government. Even so, it appears that for many residents the very real threat to their community hung over their lives for 25 years or more. As one resident said, "they [the City Council] had previously destroyed St. Ebbes and other areas… there was no reason not to expect them to destroy East Oxford." Even if the Council did make some efforts to improve the area during this period of uncertainty, a general attitude of cynicism seems to have prevailed among residents. But the fact remains that in spite of this troubled period in its history, East Oxford attracted—and continues to attract—a diverse range of people to live in the area. Unwittingly, the inner relief road saga may have played an important part in shaping the character of today's Cowley Road.

3
RETAIL THERAPY: SHOPPING AND SERVICES

Shopping in Cowley Road can be an eclectic experience. Where else in Oxford would you find specialist Italian, Russian and Greek delicatessens, a tailor specializing in clerical robes, a shop devoted to board games and a holistic therapy centre all within a few hundred feet of each other? There are plenty of familiar outlets—mobile phones and fast food seem to command an ever increasing percentage of the street—but there are few of the uniform chain stores to be found in every British high street. Instead, this is a street of small, independent shops, with a strong emphasis on multi-cultural retailing and "alternative" services.

Business activity is spread over the first half of Cowley Road, from the Plain to Divinity Road, and after Magdalen Road the street becomes more residential in nature, with only a few commercial enterprises. This is a very similar pattern to that of the 1950s. But then, however, there were also other shopping facilities in the district; Joan Parchment recalls that Bullingdon Road was also well supplied with shops of different kinds.

Cowley Road did not just provide shops, it also accommodated small businesses and public and health services. These services developed in line with demand from the community and in response to society's changing requirements. As different people came to live in the area, businesses adapted to such changes.

In 1950 there was a large variety of shops and businesses on Cowley Road, as well as some light manufacturing industries and professional and health services. As well as food shops, confectioners, drapers and house furnishers, there were also clothes and bicycle shops. Alongside these were a small number of cafés and snack bars and one or two radio rental places. "Absolutely brilliant—you could get anything you want on the Cowley Road," is how one resident sums up the street for shopping then, despite the frugality of the time. The area had something of a village atmosphere and there was also a social dimension to shopping. One resident explains why shopping could be a time-consuming activity: "You met all your friends and stopped to catch up with everybody's news... my husband dreaded it—it took so long!" Another comments: "There was no need to go into town, everything could be got on the Cowley Road… we had hat shops, wool shops, haberdasheries, pram shops, we did not need to travel."

These retail outlets represented a micro-picture of society at the time, reflecting the needs of the local community, which were similar to those nationally. The following table shows the combination of shops, services and businesses on Cowley Road during the 1950s. It gives an idea of the distribution of and variety of shops and services along the road (light industry is not included.)

BUSINESSES AND SERVICES IN COWLEY ROAD, 1950s	No.
Clothing stores (including children's clothes, shoe and boot shops and milliners)	18
Bookshops	1
Banks	2
Cycle shops	6
Churches	4
Eating houses and take-away restaurants	9
Hairdressers	8
Food stores (including butchers, grocers, fruiterers and bakers)	36
Dry cleaners	4
House furnishings (linens, drapers, upholsterers)	9
Confectioners	10
Car collection	2
Medical services (doctors, dentists, chemists, opticians, chiropodists and health service centre)	11
Pubs	5
Wine and beer stores	3
Police stations (sub)	2
Schools (including School of Technology)	4
Newsagents	4

(The police stations listed in Kelly's Directory were not as we know them today.)

FOOD SHOPS

Local greengrocers and corner shops were a typical sight in 1950s Britain, and Cowley Road was no exception. The grocers' shops were placed in conven-

ient locations for those living in neighbouring streets, and people had their
favourites. There was a wide selection of
small food shops spread along the road,
some with their own speciality such as
fruiterers or bakers, while others were
more general; there were also multi-purpose shops that doubled up as post
offices. At this time there were no supermarkets. The Coop (now the Carling
Academy) had a number of shops linked
together, such as a butcher, grocer,
chemist, gentleman's outfitter, furnishing
outlet and shoe shop, and was known as
the Coop Arcade, which was closed off
by a folding metal grille at night.
According to one mischievous individual—now very grown up—the echoing
arcade made this an excellent place to
throw penny bangers.

There were seven butchers (including the Coop); most were placed very
close together between Marston Street and Randolph Street, while one was
further along on the other side just before Glanville Road. Apparently there
was even a local slaughterhouse next to the Rat Hole pub (now the
Brickworks). Two fishmongers serviced the area, one opposite Tesco, and
another at the Plain end of the road.

Food shopping patterns were completely different then, with people
tending to shop locally and more frequently as fewer owned cars. In the early
1950s there were also shortages following the Second World War and
rationing, which ended in 1954. Refrigerators in the home were a rarity, and
storage of perishable food was a problem, making frequent shopping trips necessary. The number of butchers is a reminder that fridge owners were in a
minority at this time.

Although there were many local firms established along Cowley Road,
there were also branches of national chain stores such as Liptons and Home
and Colonial Stores, both of which originated in the late nineteenth century.
Corner shops had a more personal feel, often acting as a focal point in the
community. People would also have their favourite shops for particular prod-

ucts. For example, one family would regularly purchase their potatoes from a small greengrocers at the bottom of Cowley Road because "they sold good spuds, even thought they came with generous amounts of mud on them!" Another family did not like shopping at Liptons as they considered it "common". As people shopped more often the shopkeepers usually got to know their regular customers well. Children were regularly sent "up the road" to Liptons or the Coop and became well known too.

Convenience foods were not an option at this time, and there was little demand for exotic international food. There was one place called Hoares, which was "a high-class shop that was a bit like a deli where you could buy things a bit special," remembers Kath, who has lived in the neighbourhood for eighty years. She also recalls the bakers who made wonderful cakes and bread.

TESCO

By the end of the 1960s there were still plenty of individual grocery shops, but supermarkets had arrived and were beginning to threaten their livelihood. The first supermarket in Cowley Road was Tesco, which opened in 1962. Originally the store, now on the corner of Chapel Street, occupied a smaller space at no. 159-161, previously the site of Dennes furniture shop. On one side was the Shoppers Market Departmental Store (previously a Butlers establishment) and on the other Butlers, a food shop. (Butlers also became a supermarket about the same time as Tesco.)

Supermarkets were a completely different type of shop from the traditional grocers' shops, introducing self-service, high-volume stocking and glossy marketing. This shopping innovation coincided with the rise of commercial television and the general development of marketing. Advertisements for the new Tesco appeared in the local press in July 1962, promoting the "brand new money saving Tesco Supermarket". With over 4,000 branded lines at cut prices, the store was open for family shopping nights every Friday until 7.30pm. These advertisements were effectively the beginning of a competitive price-war culture in this part of town.

Trading stamps were introduced in some supermarkets and other places such as garages in the early 1960s. These stamps were given as a reward to customers, and could be collected and then exchanged for gifts (most required a great many stamps!) The idea of Green Shield Stamps became quite a phenomenon. A wacky 1960s band The Bonzo Dog Doo-Dah Band even wrote a song about Green Shield Stamps in 1965 on its *Gorilla* album. Tesco offered

Green Shield Stamps to its customers. By 1968 a Green Shield Stamp shop had opened on Cowley Road—now the home of Blockbuster.

Regardless of these ins and outs, one local woman found Green Shield Stamps a good firm to work for: "there were lots of social events and after five years service you went to a top hotel to meet the boss, who was a very nice person who made you feel important." The business also provided significant employment for local people.

The Coop had its own dividend scheme, which had been running for several decades, and indeed trading stamps too. Yet for some people the lure of cut prices and trading stamps was negligible as they considered that Tesco goods were inferior to those sold at Butlers and continued to patronize Butlers. Tesco modernized its store in 1970 and the *Oxford Times* reported the grand re-opening in August as follows:

> There was a piper skirting away, children with Green Shield balloons and housewives holding empty bags outside the modernised Tescos supermarket yesterday but no David Jacobs, who was to perform the re-opening ceremony. Just when smiles were beginning to crack in the light drizzle the broadcaster and former disc jockey drew up in a balloon decked car to the sound of the Skye Boat song. He sipped a glass of sherry and smashed a record with a hammer which released the red ribbon across the entrance, determined shoppers grabbed wire baskets, downed their sherry, shook Mr Jacobs hand and made for the shelves... It is now nearly three times as large.

This modernization was just the beginning. Eventually Tesco took over other buildings such as Butlers in the late 1970s and it is now a much bigger store (occupying nos. 153-167). Frequented by many locals, it continues to sell cut-price goods attractive to those on low incomes and students, but now instead of Green Shield Stamps it offers a loyalty card. In 2002 it became a Tesco Metro, the inner-city version of the out-of-town giant that stands by the eastern ring road.

GROWING DIVERSITY

One marked development during the 1970s was changing ownership of the smaller grocery stores, as many were now run by members of the ethnic communities. Raja Brothers at no. 230, now the Aziz restaurant, was one of the first of these and was opened in 1968. The store was widely welcomed as it

sold exotic produce otherwise lacking in the area and attracted a wide range of customers. Although the fundamental need was to ensure provision for the ethnic community (see below), eating patterns more generally had also begun to change, and as a result people were demanding more non-traditional produce. A delicatessen had been established on the corner of Bullingdon Road, once home to a butcher, in the late 1960s. Delicatessens sold a wider range of imported food than most supermarkets, and the success of this shop was another sign of changing eating preferences.

An altogether non-mainstream shop, Uhuru, which means "freedom" in Swahili, opened at no. 35 in 1973. (Readers may remember that this house was a cause for controversy back in the 1950s when the owner wanted to enlarge his property and permission was refused by the Council due to the planned redevelopment programme.) Uhuru was formed as a collective by a group of students involved in Third World First, a campaigning development organization. Originally the collective sold handicrafts imported from Third World cooperatives in places such as Tanzania, and was an early fair-trade enterprise. Soon after Uhuru opened, its members were approached by a local macrobiotic food society which needed a base, and the collective was able to offer one. This is apparently how "wholefoods" came to be sold there, and Uhuru was probably the first shop in the road to sell sold health food products. Fair-trade coffee was sold later on and was part of a campaign to highlight world development issues. When Uhuru first opened, customers had to bring their own paper bags to take home their purchases. As more people turned to alternative lifestyles, this increased the popularity of the shop.

One of the intentions of the collective was to open a café that would resemble a nineteenth-century coffee house but with a slant towards Third World issues. Selling handicrafts and wholefoods was easier to organize, so the café did not open until 1975 and remained open until the early 1980s. Eventually the shop moved to the other side of the road, where it continues to sell wholefoods, even if the greater availability of such products, including from supermarkets, now makes Uhuru less unusual than it was in the 1970s. But Uhuru has a remarkable history and warrants a more detailed description of its role on Cowley Road, which is given later in this book.

Today one of the most attractive features of Cowley Road is the diversity of its shopping. Although the quantity of food shops has diminished since the 1950s, the variety of goods has increased spectacularly. Much of this diversity can be attributed to the international flavour of the road. One gentleman I spoke to felt that "Asian shopkeepers still represent real shops and sell real food," therefore retaining the character of Cowley Road.

In fact, many of the grocery shops along Cowley Road are run by people from the Asian community. A visit to one of these shops such as the Eastern and Continental Stores can be an educational experience, as the range of produce from different countries is impressive. Shelves are stocked up to the

ceiling with interesting items such as salted dried fish, bunches of fresh coriander, yams and Brazilian coffee packed in the Lebanon. The freezers are full of specialist Asian goods, while unusual fruit and vegetables are on sale, as are toiletries and household products specifically aimed at the Asian community. A butcher's department sells Halal meat purchased from suppliers in Birmingham. Other produce comes from different suppliers in London.

There are several other grocers that sell similar produce, with displays of fruit and vegetables outside. Each of these shops has developed its own clientele in a very similar way to grocers in the past. Some people do all their shopping in these stores, as so much variety is available. One woman sums up the benefits of living and shopping in Cowley Road in these terms: "It is wonderful that you can go down the road and buy special vegetables, spices and herbs from one shop to make an Indian meal; walk just a bit further and you can get Italian, Russian, or Greek specialities from the delis. Where else can you do this all within twenty minutes?" She is probably speaking for many who appreciate the versatility and cosmopolitan nature of food shopping on Cowley Road. Today, it is probably unnecessary to go into Oxford's town centre for food shopping, just as was the case fifty years ago.

HOUSEHOLD ITEMS

In the 1950s quite a few shops provided goods for the household. Some specialized in selling furniture, while others included items such as drapes and linen. A few shops stretched over a number of properties and were in actual fact department stores, or akin to them. These included Hugh Wylie Ltd., a drapers and furnishers (now Shirtworks); next door (59-65) was Leonard Hughes Ltd., a drapers, outfitters and house furnishers whose premises now house a mosque and Beeline Bicycles. Capes store, which extended over three properties (86-90, next to Mango's), was listed in the street directory as a drapers, but known locally as a department store. Watching the elaborate payment arrangements at this store—involving a central cash desk and a wire and pulley system for the transactions and returning receipts and change—often made shopping more interesting for children, recalls one gentleman.

Dennes Furniture (159-161), now part of Tesco, sold house furniture and was also a drapers, and part of the existing Tesco site was once Butler's Drapery and Shoe Stores, a drapers, furnishers, outfitters and shoe store. A little further along. just past Chapel Street, was the Home Linens shop (175-177), and several other smaller shops were classified as drapers dotted along either side of the road. Andrews Furnishers at no. 38 (Bridget Wheatley Jewellery today) sold house furnishings but also had a workshop and a second-hand department. No. 232, a grocer now, was previously a credit drapers.

A few changes in the shops supplying house furnishings were evident by the end of the 1960s. Capes was still there, but Hugh Wylie had disappeared, as had Dennes Furniture, replaced by Neils Furnishers. Other new furnishing stores had opened such as Pascalls Whitewood Centre (now Café Coco). This firm had two other furniture shops further up the road at no. 176 (the Rice Box) and no. 164 (now a pawnbroker). Another expanding business was Nu-Homes, which had two properties at no. 34 (previously a tailors and now Eau de Vie) and no. 156-158 (previously the bed centre). Goodwoods was also a newly established home furnishings store occupying no. 236-238. Pascalls and Nu-Homes had extended their trade with carpet fitting services. Two new specialist floor covering shops had also opened: Mays (this remained until the late 1990s, was previously a bakery, and is now Cycle King's premises) and Variety Floors (263). Mays Carpet Store had a reputation in the immediate locality for "catching fire with monotonous regularity—smouldering carpets were very smelly." As well as the upholsterers at no. 241 which had existed in the previous decade, another was Loose Covers and Soft Furnishings at no. 106. Leonard Hughes was still trading then as drapers, as were Home Linens. There was only one new addition to this provision: John Blundells, on the corner of East Avenue, now Spires furniture shop.

The most obvious change at this juncture was the increase of house furnishing shops such as Pascalls, Nu-Homes and Neils. Carpet specialists were also becoming more popular, due in large part to the rise of home ownership, increased earning power and changing fashions in the home. But by the end of the 1970s house furnishing shops were beginning to decrease on the road, as were the drapers stores. Capes had gone, and only two remained in 1976: Leonard Hughes and John Blundells. During the 1980s and 1990s these house furnishing shops also disappeared. A pine furniture shop opened where Honest Stationery now is, but moved out in the 1990s. Today (2008) only two furniture shops are present on the road. A futon shop closed recently and a bed shop opposite Tesco also closed down within the last five years.

Second-hand furniture shops appeared on the road around the early 1960s and should be mentioned alongside those selling conventional furniture. Initially there was only one, at the bottom of Cowley Road, but by 1976 there were at least four, plus a second-hand tool shop. The increase of this type of shop was probably due to the economic recession that began to affect the country from the early 1970s, when a growing segment of consumers were unable to afford new furniture. Multi-occupation houses were also becoming more common in the area, and it was likely that landlords equipped these houses with second-hand furniture. Changing styles in interior design, with a trend for furnishing homes with "junk shop" items, particularly in older Victorian properties, were especially prevalent in the area. The second-hand shops remained on Cowley Road until 2000 but there are none left today. Their demise is a symptom of increased affluence, the availability of cheap self-assembly furniture and the popularity of car boot sales.

IRONMONGERS

There were four ironmonger shops at the end of the 1950s, but a decade later there were two remaining. One of them was Betts on the corner of Crown Street, (now Eastern and Continental Stores) which was a family business. This shop stocked the most obscure products and is remembered with fondness by former customers, some of whose memories follow:

> "In the fifties it was run by two ageing white-haired sisters (Elsie and Reenie) and by an even older man with I think a wooden leg…"
>
> "Staff were so friendly and helpful, always knew what you needed, however badly you described your request."
>
> "… things were sold in ones not packs of fives and tens."
>
> "Someone came in once and asked if they had a feeding trough for chickens, people kept livestock then you know, and she replied 'got feeding troughs for cows if you want it!' There was nothing your couldn't get at Betts."
>
> "Betts was a wonderful shop, there was a bell on entry. Once a student came to enquire if they had an archaeologist's hammer… they found one after a while searching."
>
> "It had a lovely smell of paraffin as soon as you opened the door."

Without doubt Betts was extremely popular with residents for its service and idiosyncrasies.

Ironmongers often stocked a variety of goods associated with home needs and DIY. Shergolds (later Carpenters), on the corner of Chapel Street until the 1990s, sold anything from kitchen utensils and garden furniture to crockery and wallpaper paste, enabling people to shop locally. There were also two wallpaper shops (one was near the Hi-Lo restaurant and the other is now occupied by MCM Computers at no. 148), and these remained throughout the

1950s and 1960s. Reeves DIY supplies had moved into the site of the present-day Mango's in 1972. At this time, home ownership was beginning to increase interest in DIY, with better and brighter materials popularized by television and magazine coverage.

There are no DIY shops remaining in Cowley Road today, again the result of competition from out-of-town stores. Miscellaneous household items can still be purchased from two stores, Fred's and Poundwise, which sell some of the products that ironmongers would have done in the past. There are also still a few remaining ironmongers in the city; fortunately for East Oxford residents, one of these, Silvester's Stores, is to be found in Magdalen Road, with a huge range of items, everyday and esoteric, as well as a smell of paraffin. Hopefully they will be continue to valued for their versatility, an important quality lacking in some of today's shops.

CLOTHES

Opportunities for buying clothes on Cowley Road were plentiful in the 1950s. Not only were there typical clothing stores, but there were also specialists such as milliners, tailors, hosiers and gown shops. Rationing had affected clothing supply, but even so the range of outlets suggests that it was a thriving retail sector. As we have seen, multi-purpose stores were common, and clothing departments were sometimes included within other shops. Hugh Wylie has already been identified as a house furnishers and drapers, but it was also an outfitter, as was Butler's Drapery and Shoe Stores and Albert George Morse (now Oliver James estate agents), a draper, tailor and outfitter. Another multi-purpose shop was Mrs. Millard's (now Amy's Nails), which sold ladies' and children's clothes as well as being a wool store. Oxford Bargain Stores was described as an outfitters and government surplus stores dealers.

On the corner of James Street and Cowley Road was White Brothers, another, bigger outfitters. The shop window was dressed with displays of chefs' uniforms, an indication that the area was home to many college servants. Uniforms for Cowley St. John and East Oxford schools were also apparently stocked at Whites. As established tailors in the area, the business had often supplied three generations of a family until its closure in the 1990s. Whites can be remembered for its traditional expertise in tailoring: "you walked in and they knew what size you took." Smaller tailors existed, too, such as those at no. 34 which was a ladies' and gentlemen's tailors, and no. 195.

Apart from the hosiery shop at no. 76 (now an internet café) two shops specialized as women's outfitters: Seatons (currently a Chinese medicine shop) and Estelle's (shared by Professional Music Technology and Blockbuster), and men had the option to shop at no. 54 (ironically now the Private Shop), which was listed as Hadley's Modern Man Shop. Another ladies' shop stood between Marston Street and James Street with a window display of knickers (nothing like today's fashions), which according to one resident, provided a great source of amusement for giggly little boys passing by.

Shoes or boots could be purchased at Butler's shoe department and other smaller shops, and there were at least two cobblers in Cowley Road. Milwards, (just past present-day Cycle King) had a "fun x-ray machine through which you could watch your toes wriggle" in the 1950s. Children tended to jump on and off these machines as they were quite a novelty for many, but concerns over health risks resulted eventually in them being discarded. Mr. Purves' grandfather, who lived on Cowley Road, made boots and had a workshop at the back of his house. At one time people would purchase shoes or boots that would last for years and needed mending rather than replacing. Boot-making was another example of the local enterprise. The demise of this trade began when rubber-soled footwear became mass produced.

Four shops catered for children and babies. Only one of them, Nichols (Powells and Honest Stationery) specialized in baby care. The others, Elsie Holloway (Thai Restaurant) and Babyland (now Uhuru), combined children's outfitting and baby care, while Millards joint venture has already been mentioned.

Tracking the history of clothing shops on Cowley Road follows an interesting path. While there is no doubt that the quantity of outlets diminished in the 1960s, especially as the bigger stores closed down, ultimately some new businesses opened, competing with the developing high street fashions. There was even a bridal centre in the 1970s, where the Rice Box restaurant is now. Traditional outfitters such as Hadleys and White Brothers remained for some time, and some rather unexciting stores opened. But a designer called Mabbs opened up a shop at no. 102 (Lyttons Letting Agency) and sold unusual women's clothes. Further up the road a boutique fashionably named Shaft sold stylish clothes in the early 1970s for both men and women. Loon pants, trousers with enormous flares, could be purchased for just over £2 a pair, a must for the fashion conscious, even if people have vivid memories of having to lie down on a bed to zip themselves into extremely tight loons and not being able to visit the lavatory all night. Gradually, other shops such as New Trend Boutique (opposite Manzil Way) and Lace Ups opened (now Subway), selling clothes and accessories in alternative styles.

Sadly, there are few clothes shops on the road now: Bead Games offer recycled clothes of varying condition; the Bombay Emporium, a few doors away, also offers a selection of alternative clothes; and there was until 2007 a very fashionable designer shop called Uniikki. There are, however, no children's clothing shops in the area. It seems that the main shopping centres have claimed this trade.

TRANSPORT

Horse tramways were one of the original means of public transport in Oxford. The City of Oxford & District Tramway Company was set up after the 1879 Oxford Tramways Order. Despite opposition from university members, Magdalen Bridge was widened to accommodate a four-foot gauge track for

the tramway. From 1 December 1881, the tramway ran from Magdalen Road cricket grounds to the railway station via Cowley Road, the Plain, High Street, Carfax, Queen Street and New Road. Later, other routes were opened in the city. The main depot was in Leopold Street, and one of the secondary depots was at the Cape of Good Hope on the Plain.

Plans were made for electric trams in the city, but these generated much controversy, especially with regard to overhead power lines and public ownership. By 1913 it was clear to the Council that residents wanted buses to be provided, as they were fast becoming a popular form of public transport nationally. Although he was refused permission from the Council to operate Daimler motor buses in 1913, William Morris started a bus service from Cowley Road to the station, which took ten minutes. Passengers had to pay in coupons purchased from local shops, as the licence had been refused. Another company, the Tramway Company (earlier this firm had been set to run the electric trams in the city) started to run a service in competition with Morris. Eventually the services amalgamated and became the City of Oxford Motor Services (COMS) in 1921. The COMS garage and depot was opened at no. 391 in 1924. This site was next to the home of Henry Taunt (1842-1922), a celebrated local photographer. Opposite was a recreation ground, until council houses were built in 1922.

Buses have provided the main form of public transport in Cowley Road since 1913, and have traditionally provided a reasonably reliable service as the street is on a major route in and out of the city and, different bus services pass along it. The City of Oxford Motor Services had their depot on Cowley Road for decades. Quite a few facilities were provided for the employees of COMS, which was run by the City Council. At one time the bus company had its own sports ground next to the depot and there was a hostel too. The bus depot was demolished in 2004 and the site is being re-developed for housing. Red buses were a familiar sight going up and down the street to different destinations. Once deregulation was enforced following the 1985 Transport Act, it was made much easier for private companies to set up bus services. Some residents consider there has been an improved service but others think that there are too many buses and that they contribute to environmental damage.

Bicycles have been the main form of transport for many local people and have been used for work and leisure since the beginning of the twentieth century. Many people interviewed for this book have lived in the area all their lives and recall cycling as one of the main childhood leisure activities in the 1950s and indeed beyond to the 1960s. Others talk of their fathers going to work on their bikes. Bicycle repair shops were therefore an obvious necessity, and the fact that there were six bicycle shops in the road in the 1950s suggests that there was a healthy demand for them. One particular bicycle builder stands out, by the name of Mr. Lomas. According to one gentleman who lived in the area as a child, Mr. Lomas, who was apparently slightly disabled and getting on in years, "built and maintained bikes and wheels with the expertise of a seasoned engineer, and dispensed myriad bike parts from a treasure-trove in the back of the shop." Another resident recalls that he continued to ride his "superb racing bike well into his advanced years," and also had an interest in radios, which he sold in the shop.

Bigger companies such as Halfords and Raleigh took over some of the cycle shops in the 1960s and 1970s, but today most are owned by individuals. There is clear competition between them, although each shop offers something different. Cycling continues to be a popular, cheap and easy way of getting across the city and is certainly encouraged by local environmentalists as an alternative to using a car. While there have undoubtedly been improvements for cyclists over the years, such as the introduction of cycle lanes, there is still a need for more cycle-friendly measures. Cyclox is one of the newest campaign groups for cyclists in the city. One of its main areas of work in East Oxford is to ensure that the new improvements to Cowley Road include safe cycling conditions for cyclists. Plans are currently under way for major work to improve road safety and the environment in Cowley Road. East Oxford Action led a consultation process in the community on how £1 million, from the Department for Transport, should be allocated. The scheme is run by Oxfordshire County Council and work began on these improvements in 2005.

Car servicing services expanded in the 1950s and included motor engineers. Brake lining manufacturers and motor body builders set up businesses in line with the increase in car ownership, and some of these types of businesses still remain on the eastern end of the road. At the same time, driving schools opened up as more people became car owners, and garages and car hire firms increased. Luxicars, based on the corner of Divinity Road, was one of the most recognized firms in this line of business. There were until recently quite a few car hire firms operating in the area, but not all have continued trading. Crappers, a well-known Oxford firm specializing in caravans and transport, situated further up Cowley Road, just after Cumberland Road, extended its services over the decades, but has now moved on. Nowadays the road is host to an MOT centre, specialist car and motor-bike outlets and a car body repair business.

BUSINESSES AND SERVICES

Over the last fifty years Cowley Road's businesses have been extremely varied and have included the following: cabinet makers, bookbinders, builders, conveyors, dry cleaners, electrical engineers, monumental masons, sheet metal workers, boot makers, sign writers, costumiers, timber merchants, spray painters, welders, wood turners and printers. At present there is very little light industry on the road, but there are several businesses that are run from the upper part of Cowley Road, and these include a builder's merchant. Blackwell Publishers occupied nos. 104-110 but relocated to the Cowley Business Park in 2006. These buildings have an interesting history, as they were originally built as an Assembly Hall in 1890 financed by the Morrell brewing dynasty. There were shops, a Conservative Club, a reading room and a public hall. The public hall became a theatre known as the Empire Music Hall, then East Oxford Theatre. From 1912 until 1938 it was a cinema known as the Palace Theatre. The building now houses a mix of companies and charities.

Among the professional services available on Cowley Road just after the Second World War were the following: insurance companies, decorators, financial advisors, solicitors, estate agents, hairdressers, photographers, plumbers, television engineers, tyre services, undertakers, upholsterers and watchmakers. New services and businesses were established reflecting changes in a local community. Radio rentals shops began to include television hire, and television engineers made a lucrative living. Plumbers and electricians increased in number as property was upgraded. Specialist shops serving a broader community than East Oxford itself—for example, a scooter shop in the 1960s—opened and closed as fashion or demand dictated. Conversely, businesses such as shoe and boot making closed down as demand declined in the face of changing fashions and technology.

HEALTH AND EDUCATION

Two doctors, two dentists, an optician and several chemist shops, as well as a geriatric hospital, Cowley Road Hospital, served the area in the 1950s. Other health-associated businesses have existed over the decades, such as an eye testing centre, artificial limb service, a hearing aid consultant and a herbalist.

Cowley Road Hospital, built in 1865, was initially a workhouse and as an institution it had a long history, witnessing major changes in social policy and housing thousands of inmates until its closure in 1981 and demolition soon after. Many changes were made to the institution as a result of government policies and local management strategies. After the inception of the NHS, it became a specialist hospital for older people. This institution contributed much to the history of the area and was a key landmark in the road. In 2007 a new health centre, incorporating doctors' surgeries and a pharmacy opened on the site.

There were three schools and a School of Technology during the 1950s. For the first few years after the war, Cowley Road Emergency School for Infants was situated on the corner of Divinity Road. (Bartlemas Nursery School was built later.) Present-day Leon Close was where the Schools of Technology, Art and Commerce were once sited, later known as the College of Further Education (CFE). Previously these institutions were part of the City Technical School founded by the City Council in 1891. In 1949 the Schools of Technology, Art and Commerce offered courses on building trade, engineering, science, commerce and women's crafts. Some of the departments were scattered around the city and plans to amalgamate them under one roof were under way in the 1930s but were abandoned because of the outbreak of the Second World War. The amalgamation was achieved in 1955 when the College of Technology, Art and Commerce was opened in Headington; this was later to became Oxford Polytechnic, and is now Oxford Brookes University. After 1955 some of the departments remained in the Cowley Road site, and the CFE specialized in providing courses in craft, technology, intermediate professional subjects and "O" and "A" levels. The CFE gradually moved to Oxpens from 1969 onwards as more facilities and classrooms were built.

Cowley St. John Girls School stood where Moberly Close is now, and the boys' section of the school occupied the premises now housing East Oxford Community Centre. Both these schools closed in the early 1970s, moved to new premises in Cricket Road and became co-educational after the schools were reorganized into a three-tier system. It took a while for the move to take place because the building was not ready on time.

CHANGING FACES

If changes in Cowley Road were mostly gradual in the 1950s and 1960s, by the end of the 1970s there had been more radical shifts in retailing and services. Small grocery shops had diminished considerably (from 36 to 8) and two supermarkets had opened, namely Butlers and Tesco. There was also a delicatessen, an office equipment store and a turf accountant. Clothes stores had reduced in number, but the number of banks had increased to four, and there was also an increase in financial services and DIY shops. There were more launderettes and a petrol station; gift shops were now established and there were four-second hand shops. The scooter shop had been replaced by a motor bike specialist. A health centre was built and opened in December 1967 and there were several doctors' practices in the area. Light manufacturing services were disappearing, but printers remained and motor body repairs were introduced.

Many other services disappeared such as the beer retailers, milliners, tailors, and cabinet makers. In their place came other new developments such as the Oxford Committee for Community Relations, Customs and Excise offices, the Department of Health and a smaller branch of Oxfam. Small business disappeared and alternative shops such as Uhuru, the East Oxford Advertiser book shop and an Indian Emporium selling "fancy goods" arrived.

The implications of a road running through the main road of a community had some devastating consequences, not least the effect of blight on the area as a whole. People living in the area at the time of the Eastwyke Farm Road controversy outlined how they thought the road would affect their community in a special week-long Radio Oxford programme dedicated to the issue. One of the local Labour Party councillors, Tom Blundell, who lived in Marston Street, was interviewed in November 1971 articulated his concerns:

> …now we know that the worst of all possible things is to happen—that the road is going to come right through the centre of East Oxford. East Oxford is a living community. What is going to happen is the road is going to cut the community in two and between these two parts, 30,000 cars will travel down an urban motorway.

As the development plan constantly changed, traders were understandably worried about the future of their businesses and, as outlined earlier, there was also a concerted effort by the City Council to support the new shopping centre in Cowley to the detriment of Cowley Road. The *Oxford Times* highlighted the problem of traders at the Plain end of Cowley Road in April 1976 and painted a gloomy picture with the headline "Traders Move Out": "two dozen or more shops lie empty and dust gathers thick on floors and fixtures. Painted name signs of former owners have begun to fade and many shop fronts are boarded up… 'for sale' signs or 'closing down' have taken over from shops open for business. This area, say the traders is the testing ground that will either make or break a business."

Traders considered that shops that were thriving concerns often moved to better sites nearer the town centre, and those that failed were closed up and forgotten. More businesses appeared to be collapsing than succeeding, and many premises were shut longer than local people could remember. A clothes shop proprietor explained to the newspaper:

We used to own another shop across the road... business was not too good, so we moved to smaller premises to make a go of it. But we have found it was impossible for a fashion shop to keep going in this area. Everyone goes to the centre to buy their clothes... it's alright for bigger firms who have money to cover themselves but it takes time to establish a reputation here. You have to get regular customers and the demand for a store like ours just wasn't there.

In general, it was thought that the majority of shops that survived and did good business at this time in the mid-1970s were those with specialized trades. Residents had been lobbying for the neighbourhood to be designated a General Improvement Area (GIA) since the early 1970s. This aim was finally achieved in 1977 when the City Council decided to make a large part of St. Clements (including Cowley Road area) a GIA. This meant that a concerted effort was to be made by the Council to upgrade the environment (with tree planting and pedestrianization), to improve shops by maintaining the Cowley Road as "a healthy mix of convenience, specialist and durable goods shops", and to give the area a "facelift by eradicating eyesores." Obviously this scheme took time to take effect, and some areas seem to have benefited more than others. The Plain end of Cowley Road up to Marston Street has a more "gentrified" image, with interesting shops and businesses, whereas beyond the appearance of the road is less attractive and there are fewer of these sort of shops.

Right from the start of supermarkets trading in Cowley Road, many residents continued to patronize their local stores in preference to the newcomers. But gradually these small firms collapsed in the face of supermarket competition, as it became impossible to survive the price war. According to some residents, once the supermarkets extended their products to include other items, this precipitated the demise of the small grocery shops. At one time, for instance, Tesco did not sell products like garlic or peppers. One long-term resident thinks that "Tesco killed East Oxford" because it brought down many local businesses. Another resident recognizes the advantages of having a supermarket immediately accessible in the area but also acknowledges that it has been detrimental to smaller traders. But it seems that once the smaller grocery shops became known for specialist goods, their fortunes changed and custom increased.

Although by the mid-1970s the road development scheme had been quashed by the City Council, it was still a live issue because the County

Council had resurrected the plan. The resulting uncertainty must have had a negative impact on trade, particularly from the Plain end of Cowley Road to James Street, but equally the recession of the 1970s contributed to stagnant or falling business, as did the development of bigger shopping centres

In the 1980s fewer physical changes occurred. More restaurants appeared, such as the Hi-Lo Jamaican Eating House and Hamsters, an inexpensive and eclectic bistro. A pine furniture shop, sports shops and video rentals were examples of new businesses arriving, but generally there was quite a turn-around of shop owners as these businesses did not seem to last long. The 1990s saw the opening of more restaurants, take-aways, bars and estate agents and the closing down of businesses such as Shergolds, and outlets dealing in clothes, furniture, carpets and jewellery, as well as smaller television sales and video rental businesses. Television sales and rental companies had to compete with bigger out-of-town stores, and individual video rentals with national com-

petitors like Blockbuster. Furniture, carpet and clothes stores were also up against high street businesses and the continuing development of retail parks. Some shop owners had been trading in the road for several decades and sold up because it was time to retire.

What is noticeable about business ownership since the 1970s is that those that close are not replaced with similar ventures. Most new businesses tend to be in the food sector, either restaurants or specialist grocers, and there can be a quick turnaround of businesses or ownership. It is likely that due to the changed character of the area and the increase in the student population, food is the one business that can guarantee success as compared to other forms of trade.

Other forms of new business contribute to the varied feel of the street. One of the tattoo shops, Eagle Tattoos, arrived in the early 1990s, having been relocated from the town centre via Swindon, and was set up in Cowley Road because it was the "right place at the right time", says Chris Tree, who ran the shop until its closure in 2006. The Gameskeeper, a games shop, Uniikki a designer clothes shop, Bridget Wheatley, which sells designer jewellery, Bead Games and SS 20, a skateboarding shop, are other examples of businesses that have catered to specialist interests and attract custom from outside the immediate area. Yet one trader expressed his concern at the amount of restaurants and take-aways compared in relation to other businesses: "there are very few retail outlets here now... there is not much to drag people out of town."

By 2005 a social services department and a new wave of community projects such as Mind, Save The Children, Restore (a charity that works with people with mental health problems through creative work and rehabilitation), East Oxford Action and Libra (a drug and alcohol advice centre) were present in the street. The trade union and Labour Party offices, on the other hand, had gone. Haberdasheries and material and wool shops have completely disappeared—a sign that few people make their own clothes nowadays.

CHANGES IN COWLEY ROAD, 1959–2004

	1959	2007
Churches	3	2
Mosques	0	2
Estate agents	4	9
Clothes shops	18	3
Confectioners	11	0
Newsagents	4	3

CHANGES IN COWLEY ROAD (CONTINUED...)

Post office★	3	1
Hairdressers	8	7
Restaurants/cafés	8	29
Take-aways	3	19
Bicycle shops	6	3
Pubs	5	6
Household goods	12	2
Television services	4	0
Food stores	36	15
Sex shops	0	3
Launderettes/dry cleaners	4	1
Bathroom and kitchens	0	1
Internet cafés	0	4
Phone shops	0	3

Above is a summary of changes in retailing over a period of forty-five years. Although a survey of traders was conducted in the process of researching this book, some shops may already have changed purpose or ownership as there is a significant turnover of traders. A new betting shop, video rental hire outlet and some new eating houses opened at the end of 2004, for instance.

Nevertheless, an overall impression emerges from the statistics, and changes in the road can be summed up as gains (not necessarily appreciated by everybody) and losses. In terms of gains, there are far more restaurants, internet cafés, phone shops, sex shops, alternative therapy centres, estate agents, and community projects. An increase in cafés suggests that a different sort of entertainment culture has evolved, and some of the cafés double up as restaurants or wine bars. Eating out is now undoubtedly a much more popular pastime than it was in the 1950s. Internet cafés and phone shops are relatively new phenomena, reflecting advances in communications technology and shifting consumerist trends. The first sex shop, The Private Shop, arrived in Cowley Road in the early 1980s and was strongly resisted by feminist and church groups. Since then others have been opened, but without the same public objection that first occurred. This does not mean that they are particularly welcome, but probably that people have just got used to them being there. (The Private Shop, rather bizarrely, showed a traditional sense of etiquette in September 1997 after the death of Princess Diana when it joined other local traders in closing on the day of her funeral. A notice to customers stuck on the

door on Saturday 6 September read, "As a mark of respect, this shop will close during Diana's service.")

Alternative therapy facilities, meanwhile, suggest that people are branching out from traditional medical methods and considering other options. As there are three such centres, there is clearly a demand for such services, both locally and from further afield. Estate agents have trebled in numbers over the decades. This fact is probably no surprise to long-term residents, who are well aware of the increase in buy-to-let properties and the bane of living in areas where there are several houses of multiple occupation. Community projects, for their part, are probably a sign of how much lobbying in the past has resulted in these facilities, combined with government initiatives for areas in need of regeneration.

The biggest losers are food stores, with the rise of the supermarkets, clothes and household shops, where the chains have taken over in the city centre or out of town, and confectioners, where packaged sweets have replaced traditional fare.

The twenty-first century has certainly opened up new avenues for retailing. Shopping on-line is becoming more attractive and undoubtedly plays a significant part in changing shopping patterns, expectations and competition. Small businesses and shops have a different place in commercial life today and have to have something special to successfully compete in the local market. The bustling commercial life of today's Cowley Road suggests that many have that special something.

4
POWER TO THE PEOPLE:
THE POLITICS OF PROTEST

Cowley Road has had a reputation for militancy for many years, enjoying such sobriquets as the "Left Bank of Oxford" or "Little Moscow". Most of Oxford's political activity, albeit exclusively left-wing in nature, does seem to have been concentrated along Cowley Road from the 1970s onwards. This chapter takes a look at how and why this happened and uncovers an extraordinary passage of political history over five decades. It is extraordinary because it seems that the vast majority of local, national or international political campaigns and struggles from 1950 to the present have been taken up in one way or another in the area.

What is more, there appears to have been overwhelming support from most residents for many of these campaigns. We had a taste of how residents had successfully protested against the planned inner relief road in Chapter 2. When reading through newspaper archives to research this book, it became increasingly apparent that during the late 1960s and early 1970s local residents had become exasperated and frustrated by local politicians and the City Council. Many of their concerns were focused on the local environment and facilities such as schools, play areas, traffic, housing and community recreation. The protests emerging from these concerns were led primarily by residents, who were mostly older people and families, as there were few students or communal houses at this time. Politicians also contributed to the activity, as did the local Trades Council. The car factory at Cowley, meanwhile, employed considerable numbers of local people who were often active in trade union struggles.

As the time went by, the character of the neighbourhood gradually changed. Students came to live in the area, and many stayed on, with their political interests broadening out. There was already a lively activist component among residents, but students added to this atmosphere. There can be no doubt that the 1960s, famous for revolutionary innovations within the arts and popular culture, also changed the face of politics. In fact, the two overlapped on many occasions, notably in film, art, music and literature. Artists were making political connections in their work and tackling subjects that were previously taboo. At this time various factions of socialist and activist groups developed. These included Trotskyists and Maoists, who were part of small, if well-organized, revolutionary groups, as well as anarchists and those involved in the development of campaign groups.

These organizations were certainly well represented in the area as well as having members active within the ranks of the Labour Party, and growing political activism probably came to fruition in the 1970s. It was around this time that there were cuts in public-sector spending and national and international struggles became more prominent. Campaign groups were formed to fight against cutbacks and against anti-union legislation at the car factory. Oxford, and particularly East Oxford, was fertile ground for all such groups and campaigns, as the unique combination of the car factory and the university encouraged recruitment and joint political working.

The election of the Thatcher government in 1979 ensured that these struggles, and many more, continued through the 1980s. Two of the most memorable conflicts were the miners' strike and the campaign by the Greenham Common peace campaigners against US nuclear weapons. Opposition to the Conservative government's policies continued in the 1990s, and the anti-globalization movement took off. Slogans such as Stop the City and Reclaim the Streets represented a new wave of political activity that tied in with demonstrations against the Criminal Justice Act and the Poll Tax. Direct action was taken in Cowley Road to demonstrate support for national campaigns on some of these issues.

Despite the landslide election victory of the Labour Party in 1997, the East Oxford area maintained its radical traditions, electing more Green councillors than those of the Labour Party, who had represented the area since the late 1970s (when the rest of the country was predominately Conservative) and had been in control of the City Council for decades. This trend went against the wider national and local political profile and could indicate that the area is more politically conscious—and some might argue progressive—than others of its sort.

TRADE UNIONS

William Morris, (1877-1963), later Lord Nuffield, who lived at 16 James Street from 1896 to 1903, began his working life selling and building bicycles in Oxford. He went on to make cars—his first car was launched as the Bullnose

Morris and left his Cowley factory in 1913. By 1923 his factory had expanded and 4,000 people were employed at the Cowley plant. Morris jointly formed the Pressed Steel Company in 1926 with an American company, Edward Budd Manufacturing Company of Philadelphia and J. Henry Schroeder & Co. Pressed Steel was based next door to the existing factory and produced car-bodies. The American company and Morris pulled out of Pressed Steel in the 1930s, and this business then became independent. Aircraft maintenance was carried out at the factory during the war. A merger with Austin led to the formation of the British Motor Company in 1952. Another reorganization following a merger with Triumph and Rover occurred in 1972, and the company was then known as British Leyland. Pressed Steel also joined British Leyland.

The Rover Group was formed in 1982, and in the 1990s BMW took over the company. This brief history of the car factories sets out the different companies and changes its workers have had to work under. Others, notably Alan Thornett and Richard Whiting, have written detailed histories of the Cowley car factories, which address various aspects associated with the industry. Since the establishment of the car factories thousands of residents from East Oxford have been employed there.

A familiar sight for residents in the 1950s, 1960s and 1970s was the stream of workers on their bicycles cycling home along Cowley Road at 4.30 pm every evening after the day shift at the factory had finished. As the factory was "up the road from Cowley Road", it is not surprising that the trade unions representing the majority of workers established their offices in Cowley Road. The Transport and General Workers Union (TGWU) had offices at no. 46 (now the local Mind centre), and the Amalgamated Union of Engineering Workers (AUEW) moved into no.171-173 (The Letting Shop and the Chinese Medicine Centre at the time of writing). Oxford Trades Council (founded in 1887), the local branch of the Trades Union Congress (TUC), held their meetings at the Coop Hall during the 1970s.

While the factory provided employment and contributed to the local economy, conditions for employees on the shop floor were not so good, and during the 1960s there were many industrial disputes and workers became known for their militancy. Alan Thornett, who was a leading trade unionist at the factory during the time, has written extensively about the struggle for workers' rights at Cowley. He explains in Hayter and Harvey's *The Factory and the City* that, "The history of the trade unions in the Cowley car plants is the history of the struggle against intolerable working conditions and authoritarian management." From a worker's perspective, he describes in detail the rise of the local trade union movement and how it fitted into the national context. As a shop steward in the factory, Alan was subjected to some particularly unpleasant experiences. At the height of the industrial struggles at Cowley, when he lived in East Oxford, he was hounded by the press and at one stage was threatened with a gun by a freelance journalist.

Disputes at the factory were not just about local issues; the unions were effectively fighting for basic civil rights. Up and down the country similar conflicts were being re-enacted, sometimes a variation on a theme. A dispute in 1977 about union recognition at Grunwick, a film processing firm in London, led to mass picketing by trade unionists across the country. In Oxford there were several significant industrial disputes regarding union recognition during the 1970s, notably at Blackwells Bookshop and Trust House Forte. Many national labour disputes were supported by the local Trades Council, especially towards the end of the decade when spending cuts and economic crisis fuelled a wave of industrial disputes known as the Winter of Discontent. The Trades Council also backed many local and national campaigns such as the Campaign for Nuclear Disarmament (CND), Anti-Apartheid and the Anti-Cuts movement. An important link between students and the labour movement was made in the 1970s with the setting up of the Oxford Student Trade Union Liaison Committee (OSTULC). This committee worked together with the Trades Council.

The 1980s brought Thatcherite anti-union policies into force and although the writing was already on the wall for the Cowley factory by the 1970s, the prospect of closure became more of a reality in the 1980s. The steel industry also faced a grim future, and when steel workers went on strike against closures in 1980, Oxford Trades Council gave active support and formed a steel strike support committee with OSTULC. This committee campaigned within the local labour movement and organized secondary pickets of the car factory. As many had predicted, the next major conflict with the government was led by coal miners, who went on strike in 1984. Once again, Oxford Trades Council made its solidarity apparent and set up a Miners Support Group. This was coordinated from East Oxford Community Centre and was overwhelmingly supported by the people of Oxford. The Support Group raised a phenomenal £120,000 over the year of the strike. Collections were regularly held outside Tesco. The experience of one local resident was not unusual: "Every Friday I used to get two trolleys, and put our family shopping in one and fill up another for the miners." While obviously not all Oxford's support for the miners was to be found in the Cowley Road area, it is fair to suggest that there was an unusually high level of activism there. The actions of individuals in East Oxford reflected tremendous solidarity with the strike and indicated considerable strength of feeling against the government.

By the late 1990s the future of the Cowley factory was uncertain, despite a decade of campaigning by unions and other organizations to safeguard jobs. It was a completely different industrial plant from that of sixty years earlier, as production was automated and reduced, with some lines relocated. The effects of redundancies and reductions in output inevitably had an effect on areas where many Cowley workers lived and, to a certain extent, Cowley Road was one of these. Commentators such as Ann Schofield and Mike Noble believed that the factory cutbacks resulted in the shutting down of particular furniture and clothing shops in Cowley Road.

Since the factory closures and cutbacks new business developments have been established on the old sites of the factories and have opened up new employment. Even so, the employment opportunities provided by the car factories can never really be replaced on the same level.

THE LABOUR PARTY

There has long been an evident overlap between Oxford City Labour Party and the Trades Council. Oxford City Labour Party moved into the TGWU Headquarters at 46 Cowley Road in the 1950s, and for many years Labour headquarters at general elections were based there. The Labour Group of the City Council began to hold surgeries on Tuesday evenings and Saturday mornings at Transport House from 1952 onwards. As we have seen, Labour Party members and representatives were directly involved with the issue of the inner ring road and how it was going to affect the locality. Labour politicians acted as advocates for the area, as indeed the Trades Council did.

From 1958 onwards, May Day marches from Transport House in Cowley Road through the city to St. Giles were organized by the Labour Party, Trades Council and the Cooperative Society. The themes of the marches represented major national political issues and were reported in the local press. In 1958 the march drew attention to the H-Bomb and the Rent Act. Dennis Healy, MP for Leeds East, addressed the rally and announced that quick action was needed to save the human race. The following year 200 marched from Cowley Road to St. Giles in a downpour to the words of Gene Kelly's "Singin' in the Rain". In 1960 the placards on the march featured the anti-apartheid struggle and slogans for the abolition of the 11-plus examination.

Labour Party social events were held at 46 Cowley Road and were considered worthy of press coverage. One such event was a party organized by
East Ward Labour Party in January 1952 for eighty children, who were entertained by a lantern show and Irish dancers. Later in the year, a hundred East
Ward Labour Party members attended a social at no. 46 and were treated to a
sketch produced by Marston Women's Section as well as singing and accordion
playing. A special tea party was held in 1958 for elderly Labour Party members. Guests were entertained by party members, and memories of the
pioneering days of socialism were shared at the Coop Hall.

In the 1970s, as well as holding constituency meetings in Cowley
Road, the local Labour Party branch, St. Clements, was very active in the
area. The branch met in the AUEW offices, then moved to the Coop Hall.
It was not unusual for attendance at branch meetings to reach at least thirty
or forty. St. Clements Labour Party membership was said to be one of the
highest in the country, and larger than some constituencies' total membership. A former member recalls: "you used to have to get to meetings early to
get a seat, especially for the AGM, as loads of people would turn out to vote
for prestigious positions in the Party." Open forums on subjects such as law
and order in the area took place, and a pre-election open meeting with local
candidates was held in April 1979 titled "Save East Oxford from Tory
Misrule". St. Clements Labour Party organized a conference on Leyland and
the Labour Movement in 1978. Branch socials, usually held at the East
Oxford Community Centre, were legendary and raised lots of money.
During the later half of the 1970s and early 1980s, the branch was a very
active political body. Nowadays the branch is still active but competes with
rivals such as Respect and the Green Party, which have attracted those disillusioned with the Labour Party.

PEOPLE'S REPUBLIC

Not all political activists belonged to the Labour Party, of course. There were
several Trotskyist organizations, such as the Workers Socialist League and
International Marxist Group, which were very prominent in the area from the
1970s. Other political groups were also active at the time, for example the
Socialist Workers Party and the Communist Party. All these groups contributed
to a vibrant political atmosphere in East Oxford. Before the election of Mrs.
Thatcher's government in 1979, attention was focused on establishing progressive policies, enhancing workers' control and political campaigns under the
Wilson and Callaghan governments. After 1979 there was massive opposition

to Conservative policies. One left-wing activist of the time remembers, "Public meetings on the different campaigns were packed because of the amount of interest in them and the anti-Tory feeling, and each group wanted to put their 'line' over and recruit new members."

Certainly, a sense of the "People's Republic" was in evidence along Cowley Road. This was reinforced by the amount of fly posting on unoccupied shops and available space, advertising a vast number of meetings on different political issues. "On Saturday mornings there were usually paper sellers outside Tesco, or collections for political causes and petitions to sign... and of course there were discussions held in the street when you met up with your comrades," recalls another activist.

While there was overt criticism of the Labour Party from many left-wing sources, when it came to elections, either local or national, there was often a remarkably united front to mobilize forces to help oust the Tories. According to one veteran political campaigner, "East Oxford political activity in the trades unions, Labour Party or campaigns was nationally notorious and held up as an example, as it set precedents."

THE COOPERATIVE MOVEMENT
The Cooperative Movement consisted of a wide collection of organizations including local Cooperative Societies, the Cooperative Wholesale Society

and the Cooperative Party. Each of these was founded on Cooperative principles, with an ethos of sharing and mutual self-help. The Cooperative Party was formed in 1917 and entered into an electoral agreement with the Labour Party in 1924. During the 1950s, the Cooperative movement was seen very much as part of the broader labour movement, with a strong socialist ethos.

The Coop Hall, or Assembly Rooms as it was also called, provided another venue for political meetings. As well as using the rooms for its own meetings, the Cooperative Society also lent its premises to other groups, ranging from local allotment users to political groupings. With the institution's left-leaning sympathies, it is somewhat surprising to learn that the Conservative Party's prospective parliamentary candidate, Mr. Laurence Turner, addressed a pre-election meeting at the Coop Hall in 1951.

An example of the place occupied by the Cooperative Society within the labour movement is illustrated by coverage in the *Oxford Times* of one of meetings held at the Coop Hall in 1953. The assistant secretary of the Cooperative Society, Harold Campbell, addressed the meeting and, expressing his belief that Britain had become selfish, discussed the benefits of social ownership. George Darling, Labour MP for Hillsborough, addressed the Annual General Meeting of the Cooperative Society in 1953 at the Coop Hall. He stressed the need for the Coop to reassert its place in the labour movement, emphasizing that "one of the aims of the party should be to see that there was a real social democracy, and not only social democracy but an economic democracy which would give control of the economic force of the country to the people of the country." He also stressed that workers' participation in the control of industry was essential to socialist planning: "these purposes should be carefully planned in readiness for the time when Labour and the Coop parties would again take over the government of the country." Darling said that members should not expect the details of such a plan to be in an election programme, but rather a working picture which could be placed before the electorate. It was his opinion that the Coop, with its eleven million members, was in a position to influence national policy and he felt there was no need to be pessimistic about the future.

During the 1970s and 1980s the Coop Hall continued to provide a venue for political meetings and other activities, such as fund-raising events and jumble sales. Andrew Smith was education and development officer for the society until he was elected to his position as Member of Parliament for Oxford East in 1987. The Coop Hall was taken over for music venues in 1990 and is currently home to the Zodiac nightclub. Now the Oxford Cooperative Society has undergone a merger to become the Oxford, Swindon and Gloucester Cooperative Society and is based in Botley.

OTHER POLITICAL GROUPS

Other mainstream political groups had always been active in the area, and both the Conservatives and the Liberals had social clubs locally. The Conservatives had local elected representatives on the City Council until the 1970s. But it is probably fair to say that the neighbourhood lost confidence in them for a number of reasons. First, although local councillors were sympathetic to the opponents of the inner relief road, the Conservative Party as a whole, particularly in the county, supported the scheme. Secondly, the political climate nationally was increasingly polarized with the advent of Thatcherism, and the demographic composition of East Oxford was changing towards a multi-ethnic, student-influenced community that had fewer traditional sympathies with conservatism.

The Liberal Party, for its part, was very pro-active in the area, especially with regard to opposition to the relief road and other community issues. Liberals took a lead in canvassing residents' views and improving the environment and were very involved in anti-racist issues. Pat Clements, one of the campaigners against the inner relief road, stood as a Liberal candidate in the local elections in 1972, but lost. By the 1970s the Liberals were a minority party in an area that had become conspicuously radical and interested in more profound change.

The results of the 2006 City Council elections in St Mary's Ward were as follows: Labour 141, Liberal Democrat 173, Green Party 689, Independent 33. This result confirms that the area has a strong allegiance to the Green Party and little confidence in Labour, the Liberal Democrats or Conservatives.

THE BEGINNING OF COMMUNITY RELATIONS

As more people from different countries and cultures came to live in the city from the 1950s onwards, it became important to tackle some of the welfare concerns that ethnic minorities were facing. Not only was this important on a practical basis, but also on a political front, as race began to feature as a general election issue in the autumn of 1964. In the Smethwick district of Birmingham a candidate ran an openly racist campaign which suddenly came to national attention. A number of people consequently started questioning whether the same was happening in Oxford. Ann Dummett, one of the founder members of the Oxford Committee for Racial Integration, recalls that various individuals were discovering that many problems confronting ethnic minorities had not been addressed. Meanwhile, others were also concerned about the broader issues of racial discrimination. All these people were initially working independently but eventually got together and pooled resources. A small organization, Racial Harmony, was already in existence in Oxford, apparently providing a mainly social function for ethnic minorities. By making contact with this group, real problems such as housing and health care were addressed. Early in 1965 a meeting between Oxford Council of Social Services, the City Council, representatives from the ethnic minority communities and university undergraduates established the Oxford Committee for Racial Integration (OCRI). The organization was allocated offices at the bottom of Cowley Road, at no. 14.

Much of the early work was concerned with welfare, liaison with agencies such as education, housing and social services and case work, but underpinning this activity was a political overview of race relations. Housing and educational needs were taken up. One of the very practical issues requiring attention was the fact that Council forms needed to be clearer and more accessible to non-native English speakers. Stan Taylor remembers that a very clear priority was for Muslims to have a cemetery plot. OCRI negotiated with the Council to have part of Botley Cemetery designated for Muslims.

Ann Dummett was appointed as Oxford's first community relations liaison officer in 1966. At this time there were only about twenty in the country. She explains in her book, *A Portrait of English Racism* (1973), about OCRI's early work. Enquiries in the office were extremely diverse, even at the outset, and ranged from immigration problems to requests for language classes. Different groups were set up to work on special areas concerning particular needs and interests. A small survey was carried out in 1967 which found that East Oxford residents were more tolerant than other communities towards the mixed community. Effectively, it suggested, communities where different ethnic groups lived together were more tolerant than predominately white ones, as it was important to get along with neighbours and having neighbours from another culture demystified pre-conceived ideas.

Even so, an example of racial discrimination along Cowley Road did come to the attention of OCRI in May 1967, which in turn promoted some direct action in the community. The following is an account of events collected from the *Oxford Times* and some of those involved.

OCRI was given information that a hairdressing salon on Cowley Road was operating a colour bar. Further investigation by officers of OCRI confirmed that this was the case and members considered that the situation should be brought to the public's attention. A peaceful protest was duly organized, involving a small number of people on the pavement outside the salon holding banners saying, "This Shop Has a Colour Bar", "Any Other Oxford Hairdressers Serves Anyone", "We Are Oxford Citizens against Racial Discrimination." This resulted in a conflict between the constabulary and the demonstrators, and five people were arrested. These five were Olive Gibbs, a local resident, city councillor and representative on Oxford Committee for Community Relations; Michael Dummett a philosophy don; Rev. Joe Gibbon, Minister of Cowley Road Methodist Church; Sidney Hinkes, Vicar of St. Mary's Bayswater; and Richard Fletcher, a postgraduate West Indian student. All were charged with threatening behaviour and released on £10 bail. The police were of the opinion that the placards were likely to cause a breach of the peace, and when they asked the protesters to leave they refused and were subsequently arrested. Ann Dummett, OCRI liaison officer, was separately charged with distributing insulting writings whereby a breach of the peace was likely to be caused at the same time and place.

Lawyers representing those arrested were successful in getting charges against them dismissed by Oxford magistrates, insisting that there was no case to answer. When the decision was announced, there were cheers followed by applause from the public gallery. Afterwards Olive Gibbs said, "I am happy at the result. We have made our point. It was well worth it and it has protected the right of freedom of speech." And Michael Dummett concluded, "this has proved our point and established our legal right to hold demonstrations in this city against racial discrimination."

The protest engendered further controversy, as the matter was taken up by the local MP Evan Luard with regard to the process of the arrests. After talks with Luard and the demonstrators, Roy Jenkins, the then Home Secretary, called for a nationwide investigation into procedures of detention in police stations. The Oxford City Watch Committee, (precursor to the Police Committee), requested that the chief constable report on the prosecutions against the demonstrators. Pressure was put on the government to extend the Race Relations Act to cover all public places including shops. There was also a call for the Race Relations Board to set up an official Racial Conciliation Committee for the Oxford area. In September the chief constable's report concluded that the arrest of the colour bar demonstrators was wrong and concerns regarding the arrest procedure were addressed.

The following year, another incident occurred and was reported as such in the *Oxford Times*: "Two 17 year old coloured girls were refused appointments at the hairdressers [Annettes] and were told 'we do not want your nationality here' and claimed they were told by the receptionist never to come back as they would not be served. Two white students were given appointments the same day." This incensed fellow students at the College of Further Education, who started a picket at 9 am with 52 students. The students were prepared to picket for as long as necessary and said they would be petitioning staff in the shop and the City Council later: "they were not going to give up," the paper said, "until the shop changed racial policy or closes down." Placards read: "Black and White Unite" and "Support Your Community, Fight Racialism."

This protest was on a much bigger scale than the previous picket. TGWU members joined in, as did Oxford University students, monks from Blackfriars and Evan Luard. Students carried out a survey among householders in East Oxford that asked "Do you think it is right for a shopkeeper to refuse to serve a person because of the colour of their skin?" Eighty per cent said no; twenty per cent declined to answer. Eventually the picket ended after 43 people were arrested and charged with obstructing the highway; eight people occupied Annettes, and thirty others sat on the pavement outside. According to the *Oxford Times*, supporters cheered from the other side of the street and "chanted slogans from the Thoughts of Chairman Mao (*sic*)." A week later, 37 demonstrators appeared at the Oxford Magistrates' Court and were fined £1 each for obstruction. The defendants sang the *Internationale* in court after the sentence, then, still singing, filed out of court (which was in the town hall) to meet 200 supporters outside. They claimed that theirs had been the first direct action of this kind against racism in this country. The action produced a groundswell of support in the community; Boys from Magdalen College School collected a petition of 120 signatures protesting against racism which they presented to Annettes.

ANTI-FASCISM

In the early 1930s, Oswald Mosley, the leader of the British Union of Fascists, had established a branch in Oxford, which was made up mostly of university students. David Renton describes the work of anti-fascists in Oxford during the 1930s in his pamphlet *Red Shirts and Black*. A successful anti-fascist campaign was run by town people led by the Communist Party, trade unions and the Labour Party. Alongside the trades unions fighting fascism were other organizations such as the Redshirts from Ruskin College, the Cooperative Men's Guild and Women's Guild, Woodcraft Folk and individuals. During the 1930s Mosley addressed three meetings in Oxford. A meeting organized by the BUF in May 1936 at Carfax Assembly Rooms where Mosley addressed the audience resulted in violence. David Renton notes how prominent the Oxford trade union movement was in its opposition to fascism and adds (in relation to the 1930s), "The large Left presence in Oxford provided a barrier to fascism which the BUF could never overcome."

Around the mid-1970s there was a concerted attempt by the far right to raise its profile nationally in a variety of ways. In May 1975 the City Council agreed to the National Front using a meeting room at the town hall. This decision infuriated local people who considered it an affront to community relations, especially as OCRI had also applied to hold a meeting at the same time at the town hall. Organized by the very active local Anti-Fascist Committee, thousands of people, including a strong contingent from the Asian community, picketed the town hall in order to stop the meeting. Soon after OCRI—now known as Oxford Committee for Community Relations, OCCR—moved offices to Princes Street (where the Chinese Community Centre is now) there was an attack on the premises by the far right. A considerable amount of damage was done to the office and equipment. A march through Oxford, arranged by OCCR, sent a strong message to the vandals that this behaviour was not intimidating and would not stop anti-racism in the area.

It is widely known and accepted that when people from the Caribbean and the Asian subcontinent arrived in Britain from the 1950s, the jobs they were expected to do in the United Kingdom were often menial ones. Oxford was no exception, and OCCR spent a lot of time working with employers, particularly the bigger ones, attempting to improve race relations in the workplace. According to Anne Mobbs, who was a community relations officer in the 1970s and 1980s, some employers, such as the Oxford and District Cooperative Society, were very responsive to the issue of equal opportunities, but others were resistant. A British Leyland Black Workers' Group was eventually formed to look at these issues. One local resident remembers how difficult it was for employers to accept different cultures in the workplace, as, for example, different responses to bereavement, to which some were unsympathetic.

Legislation affecting Commonwealth citizens' rights to settle in the UK was introduced in the 1960s, and since then been reviewed in one way or another. Various campaigns were launched in response to specific legislation; a conference was held in October 1979, for instance, entitled Stop the Tory Racist Laws: Repeal the 1971 Immigration Act. One inevitable part of the work of OCCR was contesting deportations. The campaign against local deportations was coordinated from OCCR, and a joint meeting of the Caribbean Association, Pakistani Welfare Association and the Indian Union Stop Inhumane Deportations was held in August 1979. Three specific campaigns were successful: Akram Dogar, Ayesha Khan and Agnes Lal were allowed to stay

The Carnival Against Racism Committee, run by OCCR, the Anti-Nazi League and the Trades Council, operated from OCCR in 1978. Although it was a lot of fun, it also involved a tremendous amount of work and organization. It was held in August at Oxpens field, and very successfully united many statutory and voluntary agencies and campaign groups at a festival to celebrate multi-racialism.

OCCR also provided a venue for political meetings and was particularly prominent in hosting anti-racist events such as a conference organized by local trade unions, Oxford Multi-Racial Action Group and the Oxford Anti-Fascist Committee on Racism at Work. A one-day conference, Educating Black Kids, was held and another meeting, Racism and the Media, was held in May 1979. Overall, there was a large amount of joint work between community groups, trade unions and OCCR.

OCCR has an important history in Cowley Road for two reasons. First, it worked towards an integrated multi-racial community as many different nationalities moved to this part of town. Consequently, many residents benefited from the work of OCCR in one way or another. Secondly, OCCR offices were well-known as being situated on Cowley Road and were thus an integral part of the local community. Since OCCR closed in the late 1980s, different groups have taken up some of the community relations role. The Chinese Community Centre, the Asian Cultural Centre and the African-Caribbean Community Action Network (ACCAN) all work in the interests of their respective constituencies.

A NEW MOVEMENT

At the 1985 Labour Party Conference, the then leader, Neil Kinnock, launched an attack on the left wing of the party. It is no coincidence that this was when political activity in the area seemed to decline. Some believe that the combination of the Labour Party's abandonment of its commitment to unilateral nuclear disarmament, defeat in successive general elections and the failure of the miners' strike contributed to many activists feeling demoralized and essentially depoliticized. Yet around the same time, a new anti-globalization movement, outside traditional Labour politics, was already gathering momentum and began organizing mass Stop the City protests against corporate capitalism. One of the first was in London in September 1983. A national and international network has since continued this campaign. This movement was attractive to those younger people who were disillusioned with mainstream political parties.

With the advent of the 1990s, one of the first campaigns to reinvigorate action against the Conservative government was that opposing the Poll Tax. This had started in the late 1980s but culminated in a demonstration of over 200,000 people in London on 31 March 1990. The Poll Tax was introduced by the Conservatives in 1990 as a local government tax not based on property value and was seen as a largely unfair system. Later in the year, Mrs. Thatcher resigned as prime minister, was replaced by John Major, and the following year the Poll Tax was abolished. The march had meanwhile galvanized many against the government of the time. Further government policies engendered more dissatisfaction, such as the Gulf War in 1991 and the Criminal Justice Act in 1994, and campaigns against these picked up where the Poll Tax Campaign left off.

The Criminal Justice Act, although mainly aimed at restricting younger people's social gatherings, had implications for public protest in general, and gave further impetus for direct action, especially among youth, as it threatened to have a direct impact on their lifestyles. At the time, House Music had taken off in the shape of "raves", both organized and spontaneous, and the future of such gatherings was jeopardized by this legislation. In Oxford people had become active against the proposed law, and one such action led to the occupation of the Ultimate Picture Palace in Jeune Street in the summer of 1994. Dave, a 19-year-old activist at the time, explains why he was opposed to the Criminal Justice Bill and why he became involved in the occupation of the cinema:

> The Criminal Justice Bill was directed towards a particular culture and increased police powers to deal with them. The culture included those who went to free parties, squatters, travellers—this was after years of Thatcher

and Conservatism... We were leading a different life and not "joining in"...
The Criminal Justice Bill was anti-rave legislation as "more than ten people listening to repetitive beats would be illegal" and they were changing
the trespass clause from a civil to a criminal matter which impacted on
squatting. The cinema had been closed for about six months and I thought
it was wasted space and [occupation] would be a good use of space and
make a point that it should be used as a cinema... We arranged a week of
activity for the occupation and borrowed a projector from a company in
London who just lent it without questions... We went to occupy the
building in the middle of the night but a police car was waiting, but we had
all these activities planned and instead squatted in a big house in East
Avenue. The police visited this house and were obviously concentrating on
this squat, so we went to the cinema and gained entry to the building.

We were arrested soon after and taken to St. Aldates and later released
without charge but in the meantime the police had gone up to East
Avenue in riot gear and with riot vans and arrested all the squatters. The
police should not have got involved as it was still a civil matter. About fifty
people went to St. Aldates to show support for those arrested and congregated in the foyer and one guy played a didgeridoo. The police wanted us
out and put the fire extinguisher on the crowd who left the police station
but were chased up the road. Some people were arrested and charged with
affray but acquitted at court as film footage showed what happened.
Squatters were eventually released without charge.

A benefit gig at EOCC was held for those that were arrested for their
legal fees and Supergrass played a gig for them... A few weeks later we
went back into the cinema, absolutely unchallenged, and occupied [it] for
a month. We opened the box office and took donations for film screenings. The *Star Wars* trilogy was the first film screened. Council sent a
business rates bill for £3000!

Inherent in Dave's story is the cynicism and frustration that many young
people felt about the government of the time and their rejection of the
lifestyles they were meant to follow. Opportunities for conventional careers
were not always available or suitable, and those pursuing artistic options were
up against obstacles, particularly financial. Direct action such as the occupation
of the cinema indicated the strength of feeling that others such as Dave experienced. To a certain extent, the occupation went some way to reclaiming their
lives—it made a point.

ENVIRONMENTALISM

There have been environmental groups—Oxford Ecology Movement, Alternatives to Nuclear Technology and Friends of the Earth—in the city since at least the 1970s. Given that Cowley Road has traditionally been the base for many non-governmental organizations like Third World First and Oxford Development Education Centre, it is not surprising that the newer environmental campaigns also made Cowley Road, or East Oxford, their home. The Political Ecology Research Group, PERG, which provided information on the dangers of nuclear energy, was originally based behind the premises of East Oxford Advertiser. Earth Arc, Corporate Watch and Undercurrents (alternative media) are newer examples of organizations that were, or are, based in the area. Another prominent environmental campaign was that against mahogany imports, when Oxford was a centre for protests against the importation of unsustainable tropical hardwoods in the early 1990s. The campaign aimed to heighten awareness of the illegal trading in mahogany and, as part of a national protest, a local timber firm was blockaded. Overall, political action during the first half of the 1990s began to draw more attention to environmental issues, and more links were made between the environment and national and international struggles.

Traditional organized politics was unappealing to many younger people because the parties did not seem to be representing their interests, mainly environmentally. Alternative campaigns such as Earth First!, a campaign from the US which came to the UK in the early 1990s, offered something different, and also acted as an umbrella for campaigning on other environmental concerns. Its website states that:

> The general principles behind Earth First! are non-hierarchical organisation and the use of direct action to confront, stop and eventually reverse the forces that are responsible for the destruction of the Earth and its inhabitants. EF! is not a cohesive group or campaign, but a convenient banner for people who share similar philosophies to work under.

During this period there was a good deal of environmental direct action, in which people from East Oxford played a large part, and EF! provided a focus for local activists.

One prominent campaigner, Mark Lynas, was active in Oxford's Earth First! in the mid-1990s. He believes that "young people rejected the Labour Party who had moved to the right and were not interested in environmental issues." This movement attracted younger people as it had no structured leadership and had strong anarchistic tendencies, quite the opposite of the formal political parties. Activists were very successful in drawing attention to environmental causes. On Halloween in 1996, for instance, there was a very memorable Reclaim the Streets protest, involving a blockade of Cowley Road, which was inspired by similar action in London and a previous demonstration in Broad Street. According to Mark, the aim of the protest was "to draw attention to the fact that roads are for people, not just cars, and to put pressure on the Council." At this stage, there was a general belief that local politicians did not take this environmental issue seriously. Cowley Road was chosen because it was a thriving community and a large amount of traffic used this arterial road to access different parts of the city. Protesters congregated at the Plain, then moved up to Cowley Road and blocked the street. The event was covered in the *Oxford Mail* under the headline "Centre of Oxford Ground to a Halt." The article went on to report that Cowley Road was closed for five hours as 200 revellers, who also came from Cambridge, London and Swindon, packed the street. Campaigners who spoke to the *Oxford Mail* said, "it was a fun atmosphere with a serious message." Another said, "we're here to make a statement about cars and have a dance and a drink at the same time." Mark is quoted as saying, "we saw nothing being done about Oxford's appalling traffic situation and we decided to take direct action of our own." Some local residents were none too happy about the event and some saw it as irresponsible.

Mark states that once more Green Party members were elected onto the Council, they took up environmental causes and raised the profile of traffic issues, and eventually the Oxford Transport Strategy, a plan to improve the traffic chaos and environment in the city, was gradually implemented from the mid-1990s.

People worked in different campaigns, and some were very passionate about them, dedicating their lives and risking criminal prosecutions to causes such as the anti-roads movement or destroying crops in a protest against genetically modified food. In Cowley Road action known as Supermarket Sweep was carried out against supermarkets. Protesters filled up trolleys with goods, making sure soft produce such as fruit was at the bottom, than abandoned the trolleys and left leaflets to explain why people should not shop in supermarkets. During the course of the event the produce at the bottom of the trolley was ruined. There was also a cross-over of political issues, and some campaigners became involved in broader social movements such as the Close

Campsfield Campaign (the immigration detention centre in Oxfordshire), as connections were made between asylum rights and globalization.

As a result of such activity and growing concern at environmental issues, Mark was instrumental in setting up Corporate Watch. This is an independent worker's cooperative based in East Oxford that researches and publicizes the social and environmental impact of large corporations, particularly multinationals. In order to gain as wide a perspective as possible, areas of research covered during the last seven years include: the Private Finance Initiative, road building, the oil industry, globalization, genetic engineering, food, toxic chemicals and privatization. This work has enabled Corporate Watch to provide information "to empower peace campaigners, environmentalists, and trade unionists; large NGOs and small autonomous groups; journalists, MPs, and members of the public." The establishment and success of an organization such as Corporate Watch reflects the demand for such a service in the twenty-first century, as the technological and communications revolution of last fifty years has left many individuals unable to keep pace with changing political realities.

It is not just younger people in East Oxford who are involved in community politics today, as people of all ages contribute to the political landscape. Some continue to be members of formal political parties, as in the 1970s, while others work in particular campaigns, and some do both. One example of such activism is the Campaign Against Masts in East Oxford (CAMEO), a movement against the siting of mobile phone masts in residential areas of East Oxford. CAMEO has involved residents of all ages, including those active in political parties and particularly the Green Party. Moreover, the fact that all of the six City Councillors in East Oxford are from the Green Party strongly suggests that the area has a specific interest in environmental issues. This shift from Labour to Green has happened gradually over the last ten years and reinforces Mark Lynas' view that, on a general level, people do not think that the Labour Party prioritizes environmental problems. Interestingly, the area has been held up as a national example of how strong the Green Party has become locally. This has a familiar resonance of the late 1970s and early 1980s when similar things were said about the Labour Party.

The twenty-first century has clearly brought a new wave of political action and expectations that challenge traditional ideas and methods. These changes must be welcomed for engaging people who may have felt excluded by previous political practices. New political parties like the Greens and Respect, which have considerable support in the area, are also active in new forms of participatory politics. While there have always been activists in the

Labour Party who participated in direct action (Olive Gibbs is an obvious example), they were usually a minority, and in the past politicians were usually on the fringes of campaign groups, offering support in other ways. This is no longer the case. One of the most intriguing aspects of Cowley Road is the many different contributions, both conventional and unconventional, that people have made to the political scene. The next chapter will recall some of these contributions.

5
THE COUNTER CULTURE: CAMPAIGNING AND COMMUNITY

Political activity in the Cowley Road area, as we have seen, has been an important feature of the last half century, taking different forms in different decades and perhaps reaching a high point in the 1970s and 1980s. Campaigns have been many and various, and have often involved local people at a grass roots level. In general, people have supported single-issue campaigns because they have been affected by a particular cause rather than joining a political organization. Campaign groups have often been formed in response to a particular situation or impending legislation. On occasions, a political organization has sponsored a campaign, especially in the case of trade union disputes such as the steel strike and miners' strike. There has often been an overlap of interests between, say, human rights groups and political groupings. Some campaigns, such as those led by Amnesty International and CND, have lasted for decades.

Meetings during the 1960s and early 1970s were generally held across the city in such places as the town hall and the Friends' Meeting House in St. Giles. In the mid-1970s, however, there was a shift towards more meetings being held in Cowley Road. Two particular establishments, Transport House and the Coop Hall, had provided venues for political meetings since the 1950s. By the end of the 1970s they were joined by at least three other meeting places: Uhuru, East Oxford Community Centre (EOCC) and OCCR. The many meetings held in the Cowley Road area during the heyday of political militancy in the 1970s and 1980s owed their existence both to suitable venues and to the fact that many activists had moved in to the area.

CAMPAIGNS IN OXFORD

One prominent campaign theme during the mid-1970s was opposition to the Labour government's stance on freedom of information, which manifested itself in a number of ways, such as an attempt to stop the publication of the Crossman diaries. Then two journalists, Crispin Aubrey and Duncan Campbell, and a former intelligence officer, John Berry, were involved in an official secrets incident known as the ABC case. The case, involving an alleged breach of state security, went on for three years until they were acquitted. Concern regarding attitudes towards freedom of information spurred on the ABC Peace News campaign, supported in particular by the National Union of Journalists. Speakers such as Aubrey were invited by local groups to address meetings in the EOCC in early 1978.

Women's rights were high on the agenda during this time, with high-profile campaigns on issues such as violence against women, fertility control, childcare provision, equal pay and sex discrimination. Women's Rights and the National Abortion Campaign held local meetings to promote their cause. Oxford Trades Council held a conference on women's rights in May 1977 and also organized a meeting on the TUC Charter on the Under Fives. Far left groups also held meetings on these issues and became involved in individual campaigns such as the National Abortion Campaign.

Industrial campaigns were, in the main, organized by the labour move-ment, as described earlier, but there were also broader issues raised, such as the rise in unemployment from the early 1970s onwards. In the summer of 1978, fifty unemployed workers, the so-called Right to Work Marchers, marched across the country to draw attention to the fact that many factories in Liverpool were closing down and worsening unemployment in the city. The Right to Work Marchers stopped at Oxford to address a meeting at the Coop Hall in June that year.

Nuclear disarmament, nuclear power and the ecological movement pro-voked intense interest during this decade, as reflected in meetings organized by People Against the Atom and the Oxford ecology movement in general. Films were also shown to illustrate working conditions in a nuclear power sta-tion.

Left-wing political groups were regular patrons of the EOCC, among them the Workers Socialist League, the Spartacists, the Socialist Workers Party (SWP), Militant and the International Marxist Group. Meetings held during the 1970s included the Rebirth of Trotskyism in Britain, organized by the Spartacist League, Fascism and the National Front, held by the SWP, Women's Liberation and Revolution, and Britain out of NATO presented by Socialist Challenge. Militant, meanwhile, addressed the topic of democracy in the Labour Party, while the Friends of Astrid Proll (of Baader-Meinhof fame) convened a meeting entitled Against the State in August 1979 to protest against the deportation of Proll back to Germany.

International struggles were widely supported in the area. Argentina, Chile, Rhodesia (Zimbabwe) and Palestine were all countries undergoing human rights crises and liberation struggles. National and local campaigns were formed to support people in these and other countries who were fighting against repressive regimes. Much of the work took the form of education, and this was organized in a number of ways, mostly at East Oxford Community Centre. Sometimes national events were held in Oxford and hosted by the local branch. An Argentinian Night, arranged by the Oxford Committee for Human Rights in Argentina in 1978, is one example of how politics and a fundraising social evening effectively combined to support an international struggle. Oxford Palestine Campaign sponsored a Weekend for Palestine event the same year. The Zimbabwe Information Group held a showing of the film *All We Want is Freedom* in 1979.

One campaign that aroused much passion in the 1970s concerned the presence in Northern Ireland of British troops. The military occupation had a long and complicated history, and there were divisions within the labour movement on how to resolve conflicts in the province. A Troops Out of Ireland campaign was very active in the area. As well as meeting locally in the community centre, it also linked up with the national organization, arranged public meetings and theatre group productions and galvanized support for the withdrawal of troops.

There were several other high-profile campaigns in the 1970s. A strong anti-cuts movement evolved in response to cutbacks in public spending and restricted services, particularly in education, health and social services. One of the most prominent campaigns involved the occupation of South Oxford Nursery in 1978 in protest at its proposed closure. The occupation involved many different people, including parents, trade unionists and political activists, and received national coverage as one of the first occupations of this kind. Much of the coordination and public support for the South Oxford Nursery occupation was generated in the EOCC. During the 1970s it also became apparent that Cowley Road Hospital was destined for closure, and a movement to stop this was set up by the Trades Council and Oxford Community Health Council, with many meetings held either in the EOCC or Coop Hall. Because the closure of Cowley Road Hospital affected the care of older people it was closely linked to the closure of another community resource for elderly persons, Longworth Hospital, which was also occupied as part of the

protest to save it. Many of these issues overlapped and came under the umbrella of the anti-cuts movement. A Rally against the Cuts was held in June 1978 at the EOCC.

Rising unemployment, meanwhile, had raised the number of families on benefits. One of the agencies to take up the issue of the benefit system was the Claimants' Union, which had started in London during the late 1960s. Part of the aim of the Claimants' Union was to represent and advise those dependent on state benefits, such as single mothers, pensioners and unemployed people. Other similar welfare rights projects grew out of the Claimants' Union, such as the Barton Project and the Oxford Rights and Information Forum. They worked in conjunction with other action groups such as the Child Poverty Action Group and held regular information meetings in Cowley Road.

By 1980 the meetings held in the EOCC, Uhuru and the Coop Hall reflected the emergence of a different political emphasis. St. Clements Labour Party's meeting in April 1980, entitled For a Labour Council, set the tone for the decade. Meetings on industrial disputes were organized by left-wing groups. The Steel Strike, Leyland and the Tories was organized by the Workers Socialist League, and the SWP organized a meeting on The Steel Strike and the Fight for Socialism. By this time the effects of cuts in health and welfare provision for older people was hitting hard in the community, and Oxford Trades Council called a public meeting, Crisis in Care for the Elderly, to voice its concerns. Youth Against the Tories had been formed to campaign for jobs for younger people. At the same time, the Labour Party was attempting to get rid of Trotskyists who had joined the party in a strategy known as entryism. Militant called a meeting—What's the Reason for the Witch Hunt?—to air this issue in public. Struggles, such as the rise of Solidarity in Poland, continued to give an international dimension to the political atmosphere, alongside the continuing issue of human rights in Chile. Popular single-issue campaigns such as Rock Against Racism, which attracted a large proportion of youth, held regular gigs in the EOCC as well as at other venues in the early 1980s.

Other significant political themes that surfaced during the 1980s were the re-growth of CND, the situation in Northern Ireland, changing Nationality Laws, violence against women and unemployment. The siting of Cruise missiles at Greenham Common in Berkshire caused considerable antagonism, while on a national level CND became more active. Oxford lay between several missile sites such as Greenham Common and Upper Heyford, and many local residents were active peace campaigners. One veteran of CND, Olive Gibbs, had lived in East Oxford since the 1950s, and although unable through ill health to be as active as she had been in her younger days, she was supportive of many of these campaigns. The situation in Northern Ireland also caused much anti-government feeling, and the hunger strikers in H Block found support on the mainland. A local group, Charter 80, was founded, and took up the cause of Catholic Irish political prisoners by holding regular public meetings and fundraising socials. Unemployment was also rising, and a local branch of the People's March for Jobs was founded, promoting the national demonstration of November 1981.

In addition to these political causes, the older campaigns continued and meetings were held on Iran, Zionism, women and health cuts and women and homelessness. Various local and national trade union disputes occurred, involving Department of Health and Social Security staff and water workers, and Cowley workers went on strike. A benefit scam was exposed in 1981, and claimants bore the brunt of a joint police and DHSS venture known as Operation Major. The Claimants' Union swiftly responded to Operation

Major by setting up a Claimants' Defence Committee, which helped those falsely arrested and/or imprisoned, monitored the legal process, documented the findings and publicized the injustice of the police action. One new emerging theme was the role of men in childcare, and a men's crèche group was formed in 1983. That same year, a campaign against a new Police Bill to give police new powers of arrest was active.

There were cultural events connected to politics in Cowley Road. Reviews by the prestigious 7:84 theatre group and Pirate Jenny were performed at EOCC. These performance highlighted political issues such as Northern Ireland, black youth in Britain and immigration. Regular benefits were also held to make money for the different campaigns. Among the first groups to use the EOCC for social gigs was Oxford Gay Switchboard in 1976. Others followed, and by 1979 there were regular women's discos at the EOCC. Political organizations, campaign groups and trade unions held fundraising jumble sales and bazaars at EOCC and the Coop Hall.

DEMONSTRATIONS

May Day marches in the 1950s and early 1960s started from the Labour Party headquarters at 46 Cowley Road. Coaches on the way to demonstrations in London would make a routine stop outside the TGWU offices. Many demonstrations also started from the Plain. A march organized by the Communist Party in June 1971 with the themes Kill the Immigration Act, Free Angela Davis, No Arms for South Africa, assembled at the Regal cinema to go to St. Giles. In the 1970s a trend was established whereby most Oxford demonstrations started or finished at the site of the Cowley Road Hospital. This was partly due to the fact that the hospital was under threat of closure from the mid-1970s and was therefore a symbolic starting point. (There was another notable exception; a march against the National Front, organized by the City Labour Party in September 1978, started from the Regal.)

OXFORD WOMEN'S LIBERATION GROUP

The first women's liberation conference was held in Oxford at Ruskin College in 1970 and ended with four demands: equal pay, equal education and job opportunities, free contraception and abortion on demand, and free 24-hour nurseries.

Oxford Women's Action Group started in about 1972. One of the women originally involved in the setting up of the group, Katherine Gieve, recalls:

I was a student at Oxford in 1972 and it was about then that the OWAG was formed following on from some consciousness raising groups and food co-ops. We met in Plantation Road at the room in the Gardeners' Arms all the time I was there. After the Women's Liberation Conference in the spring of 74 we focussed on women's legal and financial independence and presented a paper to the Women's Liberation Conference in Edinburgh in June 74 and thence we were the campaign for financial and legal independence, otherwise known as the Fifth Demand Group. When I moved to London in September 1974 the Fifth Demand group moved too.

By early 1975, OWAG had changed its name to Oxford Women's Liberation Group and was meeting at the back of the East Oxford Advertiser (see below). Women who went to OWL meetings came from very different backgrounds, some were students from the university, others academics and women from the town with all sorts of interests. The regular weekly meetings acted as an umbrella for these disparate interests. One of the main projects undertaken by OWL during the early years was setting up the Oxford refuge for women and children who had been victims of domestic violence. For many, this put feminism into practice. Domestic violence came to national attention after Erin Pizzey published her 1974 book *Scream Quietly or the Neighbours Will Hear*, which was about her work in a refuge in Chiswick. The National Women's Aid Federation was formed around the same time and the local group was affiliated to this organization.

Speakers were invited to the regular OWL meetings, which addressed issues affecting women. There was a vast amount of national and local activity at this time, and some of the topics covered were the implications of 1970s legislation such as the Equal Pay Act and the Sex Discrimination Act. A performance by a visiting theatre group featured an industrial dispute led by women, around equal pay at Trico (a windscreen wiper company). Socialist feminists tended to become more active in these types of campaigns. Women from the far left groups were active in OWL, but the International Socialists (precursors of the SWP) had their own women's section, Women's Voice.

As the women's movement expanded and became more active, it became clearer how political other issues such as women's health and sexuality were. Splinter groups were formed to take up these causes. The process of consciousness-raising in women-only forums politicized women, and some say that this gave women confidence to be more proactive in campaigns. Often women became involved in actions and movements like the nursery occupation, anti-cuts campaigns, national abortion campaign or women's aid.

A further Women's Liberation Conference, held in Birmingham in 1978, elaborated on the original demands of the 1970 conference and added three more: legal and financial independence for women; an end to discrimination against lesbians; freedom for all women from intimidation by the threat or use of male violence. In essence, the statement of demands called for an end to the laws, assumptions and institutions perpetuating male dominance and men's aggression towards women.

OWL meetings moved across the road to Uhuru in the mid-1970s. Newsletters and social events kept people in touch, and there was a strong social support network within the women's movement. Violence against women was a major issue, and a rape crisis centre was set up. There was also tremendous support from Oxford women for the Greenham women during the 1980s, and indeed many local women participated in the peace protest there.

More interest groups developed, music being one of them, and this led to the formation of the all-women rock band, the Mistakes. Women-only discos and other events were held, and lesbian politics became prominent. For quite some time there had been a perceived need for a women's centre in Oxford, and eventually one was established in the Uhuru café towards the end of 1984 and renamed the Oxford Women's Community Centre in 1988. Organizations such as Oxford Women and Ireland Group, the Claimants' Union Women's Group, a homelessness group and a lesbian mothers' group were among those who met at the centre. *Lilith*, the Oxford Women's magazine, was compiled at the centre (which closed in 1991 and is now occupied by student accommodation). Today there are many different women's campaigns and activities in the city, but there is no one place that acts as a coordinating body.

GAY POLITICS

The Oxford Campaign for Homosexual Equality (OCHE) was founded in the early 1970s. The first gay switchboard was apparently started in Oxford in 1975. This was originally run from behind the East Oxford Advertiser. It moved to a warehouse after a while, and in the 1980s was based at the Women's Centre. The initial function of the switchboard was to give information on where gay people could meet—an important function in a homophobic environment. Once up and running it quickly became apparent that the people who were calling wanted a variety of responses from the volunteer operators. Some wanted information on social activities, others wanted legal advice, and some wanted counselling. Volunteers duly identified the need for a counselling service for lesbian and gay people, and the service expanded with establishment of Friend in 1979, providing free and confidential information, support and counselling services for lesbians, gay men and bisexuals. Friend is one of the longest running help lines in the country.

Being gay in the early 1970s was difficult, as Peter describes in his experiences when he lived in Oxford from 1970 to 1982:

> When I "came out" in 1975/6, I found a long-existing gay scene that met discreetly in a couple of pubs in the city, alongside a crucial telephone service, and what I saw as a closeted and conservative branch of the Campaign for Homosexual Equality (OCHE), the whole lot very male and quite elderly (or so it appeared to someone in their 20s). Round about the same time, some students launched a rather livelier student gaysoc, which organized some interesting discussions as well as having lots of fun. These groups were actually vital in enabling many people, uncertain about their sexuality, to come out. Being a political activist, I wanted to jump into everything and make it radical, and we were given our chance by the prosecution of our only national journal, *Gay News*, by Mary Whitehouse for "blasphemous libel" in 1978. The response from the lesbian and gay community was fantastic, there was a national campaign and a march to Trafalgar Square, and lots of local actions which all helped put gay rights on the agenda and in the public eye. After.the trial, we turned the campaign into a national political campaign (the Gay Activists Alliance, GAA) and set up a branch in Oxford. Looking back, and comparing with the rights we have gained—and the far greater openness we now have—we were still a million miles from being accepted, people (even on the left) were still embarrassed and nervous talking about homosexuality (or indeed any sexuality!), and there was really deep-rooted hatred and sometimes violence towards us. But to set against this was the support from fellow lesbians and gays, and from straight friends, that made it all a really exciting time, and one that laid the foundations for the new freedoms we now enjoy.

Social events for OCHE were held at the Cape of Good Hope (now the Pub Oxford) from quite early on in the 1970s. Later they moved to the East Oxford Community Centre and the Coop Hall. The Stage Club in George Street also held regular gay nights at this time. Gradually pubs became more accommodating towards gay people and some, such as the Jolly Farmers, were known to be specifically "gay bars". Today gay couples are not seen as unusual and frequent the same social outlets as everybody else. Yet only thirty years ago this was not as acceptable, and coming out could have serious repercussions socially and professionally.

EAST OXFORD ADVERTISER

The *East Oxford Advertiser* (EOA) was a community paper started up by Jon Carpenter in September 1970. The paper, mainly financed by advertising and donations, was run from Jon's house in Magdalen Road and distributed free to 3,000 households. Inside the EOA were articles, information and advice ranging from welfare benefits to pregnancy testing alongside adverts for public meetings and demos, placement request for lodgings for teenagers from social services, local football results, letters, planning applications, reports from residents' groups, debates, gardening advice and recipes. The EOA community paper stopped in August 1973.

In May 1971 the EOA shop opened at 79 Magdalen Road and sold items such as shoulder bags, puppets and candles and second-hand goods. Weekly evening advice sessions on welfare benefits started when the shop moved to 35-37 Cowley Road in November 1971 in a corner of the old Uhuru shop. At the time the shop was run as a furniture design workshop by some ex-students. In September 1972, EOA moved over the road to no. 34 (previously Nu-Homes furniture shop and now Eau de Vie), and continued selling pottery and clothing but also books. The idea was to start an alternative, radical bookshop, with books and magazines, mostly new but some second-hand, on sale. At this time it was unlikely that these sorts of books—with a left-wing, feminist and gay perspective—would be available in high street booksellers. EOA quickly became known as a place for alternative literature, as well as cards, pottery and, for a short time, second-hand furniture.

Several campaign groups, such as OWL, OCHE, Oxford CND (Campaign ATOM), the Political Ecology Research Group (PERG) and the Oxford branch of Shelter, used the office at the back of the shop for meetings. The shop also acted as an information centre, advertising all kinds of meetings and activities and was a mine of information when access to alternative politics was not as easy as now. Feminist writings were just beginning to take off, as was gay literature. As there was no Amazon, EOA was a very welcome and helpful alternative bookshop that stocked unusual cookery and health books among radical readings. The EOA moved back to Magdalen Road in the

1980s and was replaced by the Inner Book Shop, specializing in books for mind, body and spirit.

UHURU

Uhuru has a very special place in Cowley Road history, and those who remember it as in the mid-1970s will recall a quite remarkable place. Among other things it was a café, sold whole foods (at a time when this was unusual) and handicrafts from collectives in Africa, campaigned for the developing world, encouraged community politics, provided accommodation for meetings for all sorts of groups, and offered community service placements. The establishment of the Uhuru collective epitomized the optimism many younger people felt at a time when many people were taking up international issues and putting them into a national context. The Uhuru collective approached some of these issues in a unique way.

This brief account of Uhuru has mostly been compiled by talking to the original four founder members and from their book *Uhuru—A Working Alternative*. They have recalled the history that lay behind its establishment and early days. Others who joined the collective later have also contributed their memories.

Around the end of 1972 and early 1973 a student group called Third World First organized a variety of activities aimed at helping the development of poor countries, known then as the "Third World". The group demonstrated on behalf of the Caribbean sugar-producing countries, which at this time had a special trade deal with Britain. This deal was apparently under threat as a result of Britain's 1973 entry into the European Economic Community or Common Market. One of the protesters was dressed as a sugar lump in Cornmarket, while others handed out leaflets with real sugar lumps attached. In addition to political campaigns the group also raised money for famine in Ethiopia. This activity led to discussions about the importance of a local centre to promote ideas on development. Initially the intention was to have a centre for development campaigns together with a store where items made in Third World villages, particularly cooperatives, could be sold. In the early 1970s this was a fairly new idea and a property was found at 35 Cowley Road. The group looked to Nyerere's socialist Tanzania as a model, and two members travelled to Tanzania the first summer after securing Uhuru's premises and made contacts and ordered hand-made items from coops in Ujamaa (unity in Swahili) villages. Uhuru was opened in the autumn of 1974 and by then more people had joined the collective. This is how John recalls the beginning:

When it was started Uhuru was run by fairly conventional left/liberals, who wore shoes and fairly clean clothes, and ate meat. A silversmith set up his smithy in the store and someone else started a shelf of wholefoods. Before long the Third World handicrafts were being shoved inexorably into one half of the shop, while the wholefoods expanded. Trucks were delivering 100lb-bags of brown rice, 120lb-bags of hazelnuts, large quantities of oats, raisins and other dried fruit into the storeroom, some of it for resale to smaller stores. The shop was then discovered by people all over the city including academic women from North Oxford who were initially attracted by the crafts, then overwhelmingly by the wholefoods. Once the café was opened then the need to open another shop was necessary.

The structure of Uhuru involved some paid workers and other volunteers. Members usually worked on a project and helped in the shop. Projects were either connected to Third World issues or were community-related. After a while the collective advertised for two workers in *New Society*, recruited to work specifically in the community. Wages were quite limited. Uhuru was run as a collective (although was assumed rather than discussed) and one founder member thinks:

> …it must have been in the air so strongly. Five years earlier, maybe two years earlier, a group like ours would not have made that assumption. We were radically egalitarian—going for consensus at our meetings, an equal voice for everyone. People joined the collective easily—I don't recall what membership rules we had. The group grew. Soon there were eleven people living above the store. Some were very much into the wholefoods, vegetarian cooking and holistic health. That was also in the air. Soon meat was banished from the kitchen upstairs, and it was never even contemplated for the café. Graham, who had a brilliant streak of comedy in him, would make exaggerated trips up the road to the chip shop for a saveloy, and exaggeratedly try to censor himself from talking about it.

Third World campaigns were a major priority for the collective from the beginning. Crafts sold were purchased from Tanzania, Bangladesh and India. Makonde carvings came from a cooperative in Tanzania and jewellery from Dar es Salaam. A cooperative factory in Bangladesh, sponsored by internation-

FOOD AID FOR THE RICH

600,000 tons of international food aid went to Bangladesh last year, yet only a small fraction of it went to the starving.

Where has all the food aid gone?

Less than 40% went to the rural areas where 93% of the people live.

Food aid - a political weapon.

Food aid is rarely given with no strings attached. Donor countries, especially the U.S., seem more concerned with political and financial gain than with starving people.

"And if you are looking for a way to get people to lean on you and to be dependent on you, in terms of their cooperation with you, it seems to me that food dependence would be terrific."
— Senator Hubert Humphrey

For more information see Indigestion No. 2 by Uhuru, 48 Cowley Road, Oxford.

Biodegradable bag by Campaign Co-op.

al relief agencies, provided work for 1,200 people in devastated areas, who needed to increase their market in order to expand the factory. Handloom articles in cotton and wool were purchased from a workers' cooperative for former leprosy patients.

One memorable campaign that Uhuru ran was "Campaign Coffee". Two and a half tons of instant coffee from a cooperatively run coffee factory in Tanzania were imported and sold nationally as a pioneering concept. Some projects were supported with direct financial inputs. These included raising money for the famine in Ethiopia, collecting and selling old newspapers to support a child in school at Bodh Gaya in India and donating money to Bihar, a village in India, to purchase fertilizers. Money raised by selling jewellery was also used to pay legal fees for defending political prisoners in Chile, while once a week a voluntary ten per cent levy was introduced on goods in the shop, the resulting sum being sent to the South West African People's Organization to help buy a Landrover. Leaflets were also available to explain the projects and broader political issues involved, as education was also part of these campaigns.

Although there was a strong connection with Third World First and other international projects, there was also a move to work in a local context. As Paul observes, "Though I had been involved in Third World politics and had worked for Third World First and had been politicized by my time working in Africa, Nicaragua and Mexico, I came to Uhuru with the strong belief that we needed to focus on the community in which we operated." Members of the collective participated in local projects including the East Oxford Adventure Playground, the women's refuge, Housing Action Group and Shelter, the mother and toddler group and the welfare rights group, and were involved in starting the *East Oxford News*, a community newspaper, and in the development of East Oxford Community Centre, which was just starting up. One member of the early EOCC committee fondly remembers the day that she first met volunteers from Uhuru:

> Uhuru wrote to the community association as they were moving into the area and wanted to work with us. I remember at our monthly meeting they walked in and they looked so young and so lovely. They really were so positive with the help they gave, particularly with the children. We worked together… they were very idealistic—they had just come down from university…

This tribute to the collective shows how seriously the group took community politics and also how well their offers of help were received. Memories from individuals also indicate how enthusiastic and committed they were, as Paul recalls:

> I spent most of my energy developing links to the community. We started a left leaning community newspaper, convinced the Council to fund an adventure playground at Bullingdon Road, organized a summer programme at the new community centre and worked [with others] to develop the centre. We also started working with teenagers and young adults with problems… developed a Welfare Rights Project at the community centre and did some welfare appeals for folk.

Wider political campaigns, too, were supported in different ways. An exhibition of Portuguese revolutionary posters was set up in the café, which was used by the local Spain and Portugal Group for meetings. OWL also used the café for meetings, as did other groups like the ABC Peace News Campaign and Oxford Committee Against State Repression. Other groups benefited from the ten per cent weekly levy such as the Oxford Spain and Portugal Group, Defend the 14, the National Abortion Campaign, Oxford Anti-Fascist Committee, Chile Human Rights Campaign and the National Federation of Claimants' Unions. Some local projects also received money from the levy, Gay Switchboard and Short Life Housing Project being two of them.

New projects (some city wide) had their inaugural meetings at Uhuru. These ventures included the Free University of Cowley (January 1976), the alternative newspaper meeting (October 1977) and Community Arts Group. As part of its commitment to community life, Uhuru participated in the Probation and Aftercare Community Service by Offenders Scheme. This meant that ex-offenders were placed in the shop and were supervised by the collective. Uhuru had a general commitment to accommodating the needs of vulnerable people, but during the early years there were some individuals who became dependent on the collective, and their behaviour was often quite unpredictable and challenging. Disengaged youngsters also spent quite a bit of time in the place too.

One of the original ideas behind the café was to replicate the easy-going atmosphere of a nineteenth-century Parisian café. At this time there were few cafés around Cowley Road, and this was a much needed facility. The café was obviously a good income generator, but it also meant that a wide variety of people were attracted to it and this could cause problems. But the collective took it their stride, one member recalls:

> We had various hard cases coming into the café. Things got too loose at times. Someone found out that a man who had been allowed to doss upstairs for a night was a convicted rapist. I got knocked down by the drunken father of one of the boys who used to come round and help at the café.

The philosophy of the Uhuru collective was complex, and as more people became involved the politics involved became more diverse. What is more, in hindsight, the collective had some rather ambitious aims, supporting communities in developing countries, participating in national struggles, working in the local community, as well as running a café and shop that sold food and handicrafts. Some of the collective's newer recruits had Marxist leanings and contributed to the political dialogue by raising serious criticisms of Uhuru's ideology. Others also criticized the collective's theory and practice, ranging from the way the workers were treated to its fundamental political principles. It was hard work being a member of the collective, as one former worker explains: "We also were very involved with the movement for worker ownership of businesses, attending national conferences and working long hours and endless meetings on the legal structure of our community."

The presence of a collective of hippies aroused some suspicion in the community, and Uhuru was raided by the Thames Valley drugs squad. Paul remembers: "Cowley Road was blocked off while they did this. Their haul was vitamin C powder suspected to be cocaine and Graham's mushroom growing kit bag, which of course he had to have stashed in a dark corner. God knows what exotic narcotic they thought that was." In fact, the collective did have a no-drugs policy.

As the founding members gradually moved on from 1976 onwards, the original political and community aims fell away. In the early eighties it was a women's café. But the shop across the road, acquired in order to separate the wholefoods from the community activities, survives.

EAST OXFORD COMMUNITY CENTRE

While technically the EOCC is in Princes Street, the community centre is generally seen as part of Cowley Road. As mentioned earlier, the East Oxford Community Association was founded in the early 1970s as a direct result of pressure from the community to provide a central place for local groups to meet and because of Council initiatives to encourage such community activity. After many meetings and negotiations, the old boys' school was allocated as a community centre for East Oxford residents. It has to be said that since the 1950s other areas in the city had had very active community centres, and Cowley Road, an area which was considered to be in a bad way, did not receive such a facility until the 1970s. Even then it was not the purpose-built premises that other areas had been given, but a dilapidated old Victorian school. But the group of people who had worked hard to obtain this much-needed facility in the area pooled their energy to make a vibrant community centre.

During the early 1970s many community groups were based at the EOCC such as the Cowley St. John Playgroup, East Oxford Drama Group, Bloomin' Arts and others. The Claimants' Union was accommodated in the EOCC from 1980. Women's Aid, the organization that provided accommodation and advice for women and children subjected to domestic violence, held weekly surgeries there for a number of years, while political organizations, campaign groups and trade unions held fundraising jumble sales and bazaars. The EOCC has become renowned as a political venue and was once known as the East Oxford Communist Centre.

It is worth reliving some of the reasons why the community centre came into being. As mentioned before, a group of people had come together in the first instance to fight against a common cause—the road plan and its knock-on effects, in the late 1960s early 1970s. This turned into a more pro-active lobby that wanted to improve conditions and facilities for the community, and one founding member describes the process as follows: "It started to get more positive, so instead of just fighting for getting rid of a road and getting a school, we wanted something more for East Oxford." An opinion poll of residents in East Oxford was carried out in 1970 to canvas ideas for social facilities in the area.

At a general meeting in June 1973 the decision was made to turn 151a Cowley Road into a community centre. According to the *Oxford Times*, interim chairman Andrew Panes stated that this was the first community association proper in the area but that there had been an "unhappy history so far in getting it off the ground." The association was to have the use of 151a for three years until Cowley St. John School became available. But in 1976, after the community association had moved into the new site, residents accused the City Council of ignoring the public's wishes as 151a Cowley Road was converted into two shops with flats above and not a library. The Council had decided it was more practical to redevelop the ground floor for retail premises with, residential accommodation above, and that the library would need extra funding.

Once a building had been allocated as a community centre and it was up and running, there were several local organizations that needed permanent venues such as a playgroup, youth club and a drama group. The community centre had to generate some income, and hired out rooms for socials, theatre groups, jumble sales and political benefits. As a result, the community centre became a focal point that offered leisure facilities from the mid-1970s. All in all, it was a very active and successful community centre, run by people living in the area.

COORDINATION IN THE COMMUNITY

East Oxford Action (EOA), based in the old SS. Mary and John Church Hall on Cowley Road, was originally set up through a regeneration project to improve the overall environment in East Oxford. In the late 1990s the area (originally St. Clements and East Ward) was, according to government criteria, among the ten per cent most deprived urban areas in the country. Since then the area has improved, and EOA projects have contributed to these ongoing improvements in several ways. Ironically, however, as a result EOA is not eligible for further regeneration grants. Now it has become an independent social enterprise, with community and voluntary groups, residents and partnership groups represented. An impressive list of projects supported by EOA is published in the Community Chest grants report for 2000-2004. These projects certainly reflect cross-cultural and different interest groups in the East Oxford community.

Zoe Brooks, Executive Director of EOA, considers that changing the perception of the area is important, and that improvements such as the clearing up of the playground at the entrance to Manzil Way, have raised people's expectations. Yet although on paper the area as a whole has improved, there are obviously some people who are considered vulnerable and there remains a need to target particular localities. EOA supports the existing community groups in the area and stresses that it supports the originality and spontaneity for which Cowley Road is well known.

Looking at the politics of Cowley Road today, some of the radical 1970s projects have been replaced or have been reconfigured into a twenty-first-century form. Newer organizations such as Corporate Watch are representative of the modern environmentally conscious world and might be seen as a contemporary Uhuru. East Oxford Action, an organization that was once a regeneration project, has been successful (too successful to receive further grants) and is now a "specialist regeneration consultancy" and effectively part of the corporate system. The community centre still houses the Claimants' Union—a marked reminder that some people still exist on benefits and need representation. Paper sellers are often outside Tesco, but usually it is the *Big Issue* that is being sold, rather than the Trotskyist newspapers of yesteryear. Occasionally there are leafleters or a stall is set up to advertise a campaign. This was particularly so during the run up to the recent Iraq war. Fly posters on empty shops still give clues as to current concerns and public meetings. Residents now receive regular leaflets to keep them informed on all sorts of issues from the Council, East Oxford Action and, of course, the political parties, mainly the Green Party and Labour Party which vie for political control in the area.

A new development in the last few years has been the decentralization of the City Council, with the forming of area committees. These committees are held monthly, are made up of the six elected representatives, and it is here that local business is decided. The whole proceedings are open to the general public. An open session for thirty minutes at the beginning of each meeting gives members of the public the space to raise issues and grievances. Planning decisions are discussed and voted on in the public arena, and new projects and other relevant Council business is on the agenda. It is a chance to see the elected representatives in action. Although, this is a relatively new venture—and it is difficult to gauge how representative public attendance at these meetings is—there is no doubt that it is an attempt at open government. Maybe this structure makes residents feel more in control of their environment and that their elected representatives are accountable to them. In this sense, at least, there is still a strong tradition of political participation in Cowley Road.

6
FUN AND FROLICS: ENTERTAINMENT AND EATING OUT

A plethora of restaurants and take-aways; bustling pubs, cafés and a nationally famous music venue; video and DVD shops; a sometimes hectic nightlife. It can seem at times that Cowley Road is given over to entertainment and fun.

This was hardly the case fifty years ago. In the 1950s leisure could be a frugal business, as people in general were not as well off as today and were recovering from the war. Traditional activities such as going to the pub tended to be more common for men than women. Dances were a place where younger people could meet members of the opposite sex. Other dances, such as ballroom and tea dances, were more popular with older people. Visiting the cinema was an activity that was relatively cheap and accessible and made for a regular night out for many people. It was also a boon for courting couples who could escape the attention of parents. Dining out was not as popular as it is today, as there was still a shortage of food due to rationing, and because in many ways food was not as exciting as it is today.

Many families provided their own entertainment during the immediate post-war years, as this had always been the case and money was quite short. Popular leisure activities would include playing games, listening to the radio, walks, picnics and cycle rides. Few people had a television set, and those who did had only one channel to watch at this stage. Social contact would revolve around church or school activities, family get-togethers and specific clubs and hobby groups.

By the 1960s things began to change, as social activities and pastimes expanded. New social trends emerged, not least a teenage culture, and technology developed. By the end of the 1960s there were three television channels to choose from, pop concerts and discos provided a new form of entertainment for teenagers, and for some there was more money, enabling greater access to leisure services. Most families had a car at this time. Inevitably, different types of leisure accessibility are determined by an individual's financial means, and variety and availability have changed with the times. The leisure industry has capitalized on the growth and demands of the 1960s and became more sophisticated in response to expectations and social development during the 1970s, 1980s and 1990s. The revolution in leisure can be seen in the spectacular expansion of restaurants, bars, fitness centres and video provision on today's Cowley Road.

During the last fifty years Cowley Road has been serviced by a dance hall (Coop Hall or assembly rooms), several church halls, two cinemas, seven pubs, a community centre and restaurants and cafés. Social activity has been largely centred around these establishments for over five decades. There have also been also significant social amenities in the side streets such as a youth theatre, a boys' club and many more pubs, while the Liberal and Conservative parties both had clubs in the area that contributed to leisure options.

CINEMAS

Entertainment outside the home in the 1950s would most likely have consisted either of a trip to the cinema or watching an amateur dramatics production. The Regal cinema, on the corner of Magdalen Road, was opened in April 1937. Most films then shown were in black and white until Technicolor opened up a more colourful big screen in the mid-1950s, but even then not all films were in colour. The Regal showed many box office hits and advertised in the local press. It was in a very convenient location for East Oxford residents and was another marker of how the community was independent of some of the city centre facilities. On Saturday mornings hundreds of youngsters packed the cinema to watch three hours of ABC Minors cinema for approximately sixpence. The Saturday morning clubs were instigated in the country in the mid-1950s before the advent of Saturday morning children's TV. All sorts of films were shown, ranging from Disney cartoons to action films. For parents this all-morning activity was a godsend; as one local mother said, "it got the children out of the house all morning and kept them out of trouble!" Some children were not allowed to go to Minors, as their parents considered it "common", and felt indignant that they were deprived of this facility. Another mother described her horror when she was visited by a district nurse to inform her that her children had got nits, which they had probably picked up at Minors. Most children who visited the Saturday morning clubs thoroughly enjoyed their sessions, screaming at the frightening episodes in the adventure movies, laughing at the cartoons and singing along to the Minors theme song.

Of course, this facility was not exclusive to children from East Oxford and on occasions there would be minor fracas between rival groups. The cinema was said to have held up to 2,000 people, and those recollecting their ABC Minors experiences remember that the cinema was full but do not recall any official supervision. All were too spellbound by the images on the screen. On the whole, it was a pleasant atmosphere, and the children were kept thoroughly entertained while eating their bags of toffee crunch, sherbet lemons or pineapple chunks.

The Regal closed in June 1970 and the building was transformed into a bingo hall, which closed in late 2004. Since 2007 it has functioned occasionally as a live music and party venue. Another cinema, the Penultimate Picture Palace (known as the PPP), on the Cowley Road corner of Jeune Street, was reopened in 1976. The cinema had originally opened as the Picture Palace in 1911 but closed in 1918. The PPP was the enterprise of Bill Heine, now a local radio presenter. Bill opened the cinema because in the early 1970s the cinemas in Oxford screened only mainstream box office hits and there was nowhere showing the type of creative films that were winning awards at the Cannes Film Festival. Before he purchased the cinema it had been used as a warehouse for Neils furniture store. Negotiations took approximately three years and the cinema was finally opened in July 1976. The cinema had a striking visual presence, painted all black with a white pair of Al Jolson hands adorning the front. These were designed by a local sculptor (who also designed a shark falling through Bill's roof in his house in Headington). Al Jolson's hands were chosen as he starred in the first talking picture in 1927, *The Jazz Singer*, but there were no talkies screened at the cinema, as it closed in 1918. The original pay-box from 1911 was kept, giving the cinema an independent image. Another unique characteristic was that there was no central heating. The heating system had to be switched on at 11am in order to warm it up efficiently for 7pm, and if there was a power cut or any other hitch, then this affected the temperature control. Bill also opened a poster shop across the road, The Silent Screen, and tried to open an ice cream parlour but was met with local opposition. Residents believed that it would generate too much noise from customers.

Films are still regularly screened there today, and the renamed Ultimate Picture Palace is a much appreciated local cinema.

STAYING IN

In the early days of television it was no easy business to get a decent picture. Stan's family managed to get a television in 1949, as his father worked in the trade, but it was very difficult to get good reception. Stan remembers the problems involved: "Television then was on air for a limited time, it started at 8.30 pm and finished at 10.30 pm and was dependent on atmospheric conditions. We could not watch it unless the curtains were drawn…" Restricted viewing was certainly the norm in the 1950s and early 1960s, and daytime television as we know it today was not an option. There were occasions when there were transmissions during the day time, but these were usually reserved for special events such as the coronation, state funerals and royal weddings. As few people owned televisions, those that did shared their sets with neighbours to celebrate important national events such as the coronation of Queen Elizabeth in 1953.

At first there was only the BBC, but ITV started in 1955. Television viewing became more widespread throughout the 1960s and reception improved. In November 1955 the *Oxford Times* reported that there was a shortage of TV aerials and that television dealers were finding it difficult to keep up with the servicing and installation. Three years later, in 1958, Telefusion, a national television rental company, visited Oxford as it was one of 150 black spots for reception, and plans were made to rectify this situation. The newspaper's letters page has much correspondence on the subject, indicating the public's frustration at the unsatisfactory service.

Television ownership became more widespread during the 1950s and 1960s and probably contributed to the decline of cinema audiences. Shops in Cowley Road reflected this change. In the late 1950s television service shops had opened, some combined with TV and radio rental shops. Televisions could be hired, and for some this was a convenient way to purchase a set as they were quite expensive to buy and often went wrong. Fixing a set was complicated, especially so with the new colour televisions that arrived in the late 1960s, and repairs became a thriving industry. Today, television hire firms and engineers have disappeared from Cowley Road, as is cheaper to buy a new set than repair a broken one.

Video recorders became available in the early 1980s, and some television shops also rented them out. Video film rental shops also appeared. Several shops rented out videos as a sideline to their main business and some still continue to do so, but a few new traders opened up new shops and specialized in video rentals. This changed, however, when another big chain, Blockbuster, opened up and dominated the local market, moving into DVD rental. At the end of 2004 Videosyncratic, a new video/DVD lending shop, providing an alternative market to the mainstream films available elsewhere, opened in the road.

LOCAL ENTERTAINMENT

Drama productions have been a feature of East Oxford over the years, with amateur dramatics playing a double role in providing entertainment and a hobby for the community. Various theatre groups have been established since the 1950s for children and adults. In the early 1950s, for instance, there were several performances by amateur dramatic societies in the area. The Gladiators' performance of *The Man who Came to Dinner* was produced at St. John's Hall in Marston Street and received a good review from the *Oxford Times*. SS. Mary and John Church Hall hosted Zodia's performances of one-act plays, and CADS (a drama group) put on *The Happiest Days of Your Life* at the Congregationalist Hall. Later, further drama groups were established, such as East Oxford Drama Group, which started in 1975, met at the community centre and gave several performances there from the mid to late 1970s. Another theatre group, which although not on Cowley Road, got going in the late 1970s and became an important part of East Oxford's cultural life. Pegasus Youth Theatre in Magdalen Road took off in the 1980s and continues to offer great opportunities to local children and teenagers in theatre and dance. It was not only drama groups that offered theatrical entertainment, as local scouts and guides also presented occasional performances in the area's church halls.

Church halls have had a versatile existence on Cowley Road. They, along with the Coop Hall, have hosted many events ranging from allotment AGM dinners to amateur dramatic performances, from jumble sales to pet and horticultural shows. During the 1950s church halls provided venues for the East Ward Allotment Society Show, the Horticultural Show and such intriguing events as the Fur and Feather Society, the Cage Bird Society and the Oxford Fanciers Society's Rabbit Show. These events were well attended and there were plenty of entries for the competitions, often rising into the hundreds.

The 1953 coronation provided an impetus for social activity. A local Coronation Committee was formed in 1952 and celebratory events were subsequently organized. One of these was the Coronation Show of East Oxford Produce in 1953, where there were over 345 entries to mark the occasion.

While some of these societies still exist in different forms, the extent of their presence is not as obvious on Cowley Road. Another mainstay of church hall activity was the jumble sale, but these, too, became less common during the 1980s and 1990s and have probably now been replaced by car boot sales. Car boot sales make a profit for individuals, whereas the jumble sales normally raised funds for organizations.

CHILDREN'S ACTIVITIES

The Cowley Road neighbourhood has always offered a range of activities for children, ranging from the traditional Scout and Guide movements to the more creative activities promoted in the 1970s. Scouts and Guides groups met in the road's church halls, and there was a boys' club in Marston Street. Sea Scouts also met in the Methodist Church Hall. A former member recalls his time in the Sea Scouts as being occasionally embarrassing, as "the lads used to have to practise ballroom dancing with rather buxom middle-aged women and it was rather difficult to dance properly..."

From 1963 the Coop ran several Children's Groups, which included basic playtime activities combined with fun and learning sessions and choirs. These activity sessions were run at the education centre at 194 Cowley Road but some were also held at Headington, Littlemore and Summertown on Saturday mornings and on weekdays. The groups were known as Pathfinders and were able to provide indoor and outdoor activities for children aged 7-11, while another group was aimed at 11-15 year olds. Elocution classes were also offered, but only in Summertown and Headington, not Cowley Road! Was this a reflection on the social status or capabilities of the children in the area?

Later, in 1983, the Woodcraft Folk, an alternative to Scouts, Cubs, Guides and Brownies was started and also met at the Coop Hall. At this time Oxford East MP Andrew Smith was the education officer at the Oxford and District Coop and based in the Coop Hall.

Children's activities were campaigned for by parents and community organizations in the late 1960s. An available site for the adventure playground was caught up in the Eastwyke Farm saga. Holiday play schemes (projects that provided supervised activities for children) started in Cowley Road in the early 1970s alongside the adventure playground movement. The local authority had begun to expand its youth services and provided staff for these projects. Older children's needs were being addressed—an indicator that adolescents needed positive attention—as home entertainment and traditional recreation facilities were not enough for the new generation of teenagers. Projects at the community centre were also developing. Bloomin' Arts, a community arts project, was established in the mid-1970s and based at the EOCC. Bloomin' Arts was instrumental in many community projects, and although a city-wide facility and not exclusively for children, many of its diverse activities were designed to include children and families. Halloween mask-making parties, pottery clubs, women's art weekends, street theatre projects and photographic workshops were some of the sessions it ran. Mural painting was one of the speciality groups run at Bloomin' Arts, and the local tradition of painting walls stems from this activity. Bloomin' Arts also worked very closely with adventure playgrounds, youth groups and with disaffected youngsters. Fusion is the present-day successor to Bloomin' Arts, and although the name and the structure of the organization have changed, the underlying philosophy has been retained. Projects are run across the city and county, but since Fusion is based in East Oxford, it is naturally used more by local residents.

SPORTS

Sports facilities have never been a prominent feature of Cowley Road, probably due to limited space in the first instance. In the 1950s the East Oxford Bowls Club had a site opposite the Regal cinema, but stopped using it a couple of years ago, and the bus garage had playing fields available for staff. Fencing classes at the College of Further Education were organized for people in the community by the Polytechnic in the early 1970s. A fitness centre was temporarily opened above Spires furniture shop in the early 1990s. Martial arts sessions have been held at the community centre from the 1970s onwards. Off Cowley Road itself, a local authority initiative has provided a specialist indoor sports centre in Collins Street for residents, while the grounds of East Oxford First School contain an all-weather 5-a-side football pitch.

EATING OUT

There is no shortage of choice when it comes to restaurants and cafés in Cowley Road. Not only do places offer a wide range of different cuisine, but most cater for different groups of people and have interesting dishes at competitive prices. It is obviously the case that many restaurants enjoy healthy patronage from students. Vacation time is usually much less busy than during the term and is a reminder of the economic contribution made by the student population in the area. Nevertheless, for residents these times can be a welcome opportunity for a quiet meal out.

Restaurants were comparatively few and far between in the 1950s. Most eating houses were cafés and the take-aways were limited to fish and chip shops. There were three of these, listed as fried fish shops, and were located at the corner of Stockmore Street, near the Excelsior Café and further east, where Simon's fish and chip shop is today. There were eight cafés and restaurants on Cowley Road by the end of the 1950s, and most tended to be café-style. At the Plain end of the road was Mike's Café at no. 13, and Sid's Café occupied the premises of the former Moonlight Restaurant. Between

Stockmore Street and Marston Street were Tea Rooms (now A.T. Box Oriental Café), while further on at no. 228 (the site of the Aziz) was another café. Then there was the Excelsior and Espresso Bar (this is still open today), which stayed open until 10.40 pm. On the other side of the road, just before Divinity Road, was a restaurant at no. 209 (now Dil Dunia), and there were two cafés between Divinity Road and Bartlemas Road at nos. 237 and 247—the Oak Tree Café (now the Star of Asia) and the Fulbrook Farm Restaurant (La Capannina).

Eating out was not really a regular activity for many people during this time, as food rationing and boring menus were deterrents, as was cost. One gentleman, who has lived in East Oxford for many decades, remembers his grandmother's thinking on eating out: "you didn't know what you were going to be fed... and you could cook quite well at home." Some pubs also provided meals, particularly at lunchtime. For special occasions it is likely that people would have eaten in a restaurant in town or at one of the local hotel restaurants. One couple would drive out to the country, if they could get a babysitter, for "chicken in the basket", a 1960s favourite. Fish and chips, however, was a more affordable treat for families that could be eaten at home.

The first Chinese restaurant was the Kumling at no. 58, opening around 1960. A second was established in1962, the Pagoda, on the site of the Halcrow Restaurant, now Dil Dunia. Early customers recall how limited the menus were, comprising a choice of three dishes and nowhere near as extensive as now. But this was the time that international cuisine hit Cowley Road, as the first Indian restaurant, the Himalay, had also opened at no. 84 (now the Hajduczek Polish restaurant). The Himalay served Pakistani, Indian, English and "continental" dishes and was open until midnight every night. It seems that Indian restaurants were not very common in Britain at the beginning of the 1960s, although Oxford had at least one other Indian restaurant at this time on the High Street. (Apparently Oxford was one of the first towns outside London to have an Indian restaurant; the Taj Mahal in Turl Street opened in 1937.) Indian restaurants became very popular during the late 1960s as they were cheap and different, and many more opened later on Cowley Road. Around the same time the Continental Café (now the Star of Asia) opened. By the end of the decade there was also an Italian restaurant, La Capannina, still in existence today.

The rise in the number of international restaurants can be related to the increase of immigration during the 1950s and 1960s as well as a taste for foreign food acquired by British tourists overseas. These restaurants, notably the

Indian ones, were also relatively cheap and therefore very convenient for the burgeoning student population. All of the four restaurants on Cowley Road in the 1960s specialized in international food—two Chinese, one Indian and one Italian. The cafés mostly tended to be of a traditional English nature, with the exception of the Continental Café and the Excelsior which were beginning to serve some dishes such as spaghetti Bolognese and mousaka. Fish and chip shops still dominated the take-away sector.

Today there are around thirty eating houses to choose from. The choices include French, Polish, Thai, Middle Eastern, Moroccan, nine different Indian restaurants, Jamaican, Mexican, Japanese, Italian and several Chinese restaurants. Not only is there a fantastic choice for residents and visitors to Cowley Road, but each place has a particular ambience. All these types of restaurants and take-aways show how dynamic the road is and reflect the extensive mix of cultures and nationalities in the community. Equally impressive in culinary terms is the choice offered by at least thirteen take-aways (not including the take-away service offered by restaurants). These range from Cambodian to Lebanese and also include sandwich shops, Kentucky Fried Chicken, kebabs, fish and chips and pizzas. People appreciate the diversity of eating options, as they do the wide range of food shops. Mary spells out her opinion of the road's culinary choices: "What wonderful flavours and smells and choices there are here." And it is precisely this multi-national atmosphere that attracts many people to Cowley Road.

THE EXCELSIOR

One eating place on Cowley Road has to be singled out as exceptional, and that is the Excelsior Café. It has been established as a café since approximately 1945. The current owner bought it in 1961 and still remains in charge. Of all the places on Cowley Road it is the Excelsior Café that evokes some of the fondest memories. While the street can justifiably boast of its international cuisine, the Excelsior was serving exotic food way ahead of everybody else in the very early 1960s. The same menu and chef are still in there in 2005, offering egg, hamburger, chips and beans, or omelette and chips, along with spaghetti or stuffed tomatoes or peppers. Special continental puddings were brought in from London, and rhum babas were very popular with customers. Meals at the café were, and still are, very good value. It was a popular place for lunch for workers on Cowley Road in the 1960s and to a certain extent replaced some of the municipal restaurants that had offered good-value meals in the 1940s and 1950s. There have been some changes and additions, but the Excelsior was

very progressive in the days when people were still conservative in their eating habits.

Many people I spoke to remember the Excelsior from their childhood. One gentleman recalls calling in for "frothy coffee" (the original caffè latte) after swimming at Temple Cowley pool. Others recall going in after speedway events, after Minors performances on Saturdays, or for a birthday treat. Students from the CFE also frequented the place, as one former customer, Stan Taylor, remembers regularly eating baked beans on toast there.

Customers at the Excelsior are a mixture of people ranging from students and teachers to street people. Everybody is treated the same. The Excelsior is well known for this mixed clientele and this is part of its attraction. A community policeman used to regularly frequent the café on his rounds and would sometimes help people with form filling. When he retired some years ago, these customers had a collection for him to show their gratitude.

Andrew, the proprietor, has been there since 1961 and is a familiar figure on the road. One outstanding characteristic of the Excelsior is that there have been few changes to the place since the 1960s. Someone who travels the world observes that "it is always the same when you come home"; another customer says: "The menus, the décor, the proprietor and the customers are all strangely reminiscent of a time gone by… you know what you are getting there—it's honest."

The Excelsior is in competition with the likes of Café Coco, but it retains tradition, loyalty, value for money and character, and continues to attract a particularly mixed clientele. Above all, it is has a old-fashioned personal touch, which many people value. The Excelsior's management conversely appreciates the community aspect of Cowley Road and supports the Carnival, donating £300 towards its expenses as a gesture of support.

PUBS

Going out for a drink has never presented a problem on Cowley Road. Generally speaking, until the 1970s pubs were traditionally thought of as a male domain and women were often assigned to the "snug", a smaller room off the main bar. As the years went by, the nature and style of pubs changed, and most now actively encourage women to come out to drink. Families have also enjoyed them, and many would often finish a summer walk with a drink at a pub with a garden for the children to play in.

Altogether there have been eight public houses over the last fifty years on Cowley Road. All but one remain; the Prince of Wales on the corner of Temple Street, is now a branch of Nando's restaurant chain. Some of the remaining ones have been renamed: The New Inn is the Corridor, the Bullingdon Arms is simply the Bullingdon, the Ampney Cottage is the Hobgoblin, the Crown Tavern became the Rat Hole and is now the Brickworks, and the University and City Arms is the City Arms after a spell as the Philosopher and Firkin. The Cape of Good Hope has re-adapted its old name after a period as The Pub. The Elm Tree has closed.

Each bar has its own character and clientele that have changed with time. The Brickworks has an interesting history, and the following story illustrates how bars would attract particular customers. In 1950 the police opposed the licence for the then Crown Tavern, already known locally as the "Rat Hole", on the grounds that the premises were structurally unsuitable as it was effectively a semi-basement in a converted dwelling house, that it contravened some licensing regulations, and that there were four "better type" houses nearby which could provide for the community's needs. The *Oxford Mail* reported the hearing in March 1950, when the police described their observations of the bar: that it was run in a house that should have been closed years before; that it needed artificial light, even in daytime; and that the lavatories very poor. The business had apparently been in the family for fifty years and did fair trade, but was not sufficient to supply a living for the licensee who worked elsewhere by day. Even the police admitted that conduct in the pub had always

been good, but they considered that the atmosphere was thick with smoke and unhealthy. One Saturday evening, they submitted, when there were fifty people in bar, it was difficult to get from one end of the premises to the other.

Legal representation for the licensee and the owners suggested that the customers should be the judges of what was necessary. The lawyer pointed out that the Crown did better trade than other pubs in the area and called for evidence from regular customers. Several of these regulars lived in neighbouring streets and were over seventy years old. One 72-year-old gentleman from Catherine Street told the hearing that he never suffered ill health through using the Crown and declared: "I am still working and do 22 miles to my work." He described the pub as a "home from home… I don't think I am living under the age of dictation as to where I should go and what I should do." Another customer from East Avenue had been frequenting the pub for over fifty years and said: "We are the happiest family that meets in any public house that I know of." A further contribution in support of the licence was given by another septuagenarian gentleman from Randolph Street, who had also been a customer for fifty years: "I hope you will not take away this licence and cause resentment and disappointment for the honest men who use this house."

The Justices visited and renewed the licence but considered that improvements needed to be made, particularly to lavatory facilities. What is particularly impressive about this case is the comment of the chairman of the bench, who summed up the case by saying: "Magistrates are considerably influenced by what we have heard, and it is evident this is a house which is used almost as a club, and we feel very reluctant to upset the happy conditions which apparently are prevailing here."

The character of the pub inevitably changed, especially when landlords changed, and from the late 1960s the pub became associated with a younger clientele. The Brickworks still attracts this type of customer but has become a much smarter drinking place in line with today's standards.

The Brickworks hosted a regular poetry gig, Hammer and Tongue. The sessions first began in October 2003 and became popular, with over a hundred people turning up to a gig in May 2004. These events known as "slams" are quite different from a traditional poetry evening as they are competitive. Competitors are given three minutes to perform their poetry and are judged by randomly selected arbiters from the audience. The events were founded by Steve Larkin, whom *Isis* magazine describe as: "a performance poet, a Greenpeace activist and a dedicated supporter of the Anti-Nazi League, but first and foremost a poet. One of the most important things for him is to revolutionise the image that poets are lumbered with in our day. He is no grey-bearded sage philosophising in riddles. He is an activist who cares passionately about his community, and who uses exuberant street lyricism to jump across a range of contemporary issues with a sincere enthusiasm that demands our attention. He's the paragon of self-conscious 21st-century living." Reviews and advertisements for the poetry slams suggest that they are anarchic and unpredictable entertainment.

The Bullingdon Arms established itself as a pub where live Irish music was played from 1977. This venue attracted a wide range of customers, from those having a quick drink after a political meeting to members of the Irish community and people wanting to listen to the music. The pub is a legend in itself, and the contribution it has made to the local music scene will be discussed later.

Another pub worthy of mention is the ex-Elm Tree, as this hostelry had the first black landlord appointed by Morrells brewery in 1979. The Elm Tree clearly appealed to the West Indian population in the area, and like the Bullingdon Arms became a mixed pub offering a particular atmosphere. Also well liked by younger people was the Cape of Good Hope at the bottom of Cowley Road, as it had facilities for social events upstairs.

Although not actually on Cowley Road, the local Conservatives and Liberals both had clubs nearby. The Liberal Club was on Crown Street, and is

now Crown House, and the Conservative Club remains on the corner of James Street and St. Mary's Road. By 1975 the Caribbean Sunrise Club in Cowley Road provided a social venue for the African-Caribbean community and added to the mix of different drinking options in the road.

There were certainly many drinking options in the 1960s and 1970s, as there was also no shortage of pubs in the residential streets off Cowley Road. Political and cultural preferences were increasingly catered to, and as women became more assertive in their social life, some of venues were began to take this into account. Over the last two decades these pubs have changed in character again as they respond to an increasingly youthful clientele. Some have bouncers on the door on weekend and celebration nights, as is common in the town centre. Wine bars became fashionable and, later, a café culture emerged, the road also witnessed the advent of such establishments as Café Coco, Mango's and Bar Baby, popular with different groups of people and offering an alternative to pubs.

In a sense, the new generation of drinking venues could be considered as exclusive to younger people, and older people are being pushed out. The traditional pub image has certainly largely disappeared from Cowley Road, but it is also fair to say that some pubs in adjacent streets do offer traditional facilities. Extended licensing hours are also largely aimed at a young drinking clientele. Many pubs were owned by two local breweries in the 1960s and 1970s, Morrells and Morland. These companies have since been taken over by multinationals and production has moved away.

EAST OXFORD "COMMUNIST CENTRE"

The political role of EOCC has been discussed elsewhere, but it is important to remember that it has a social dimension that is particularly important for some older residents who feel excluded from youth-oriented pubs and bars on Cowley Road.

Initially there was no bar in the building, but following successful discussions with Morland, the brewery effectively sponsored the establishment of the bar, and initially it was a very successful venture. This was partly because the community centre also offered a range of activities such as badminton, yoga and adult education, and people would stop off for a drink in the bar afterwards. The club also offered a family environment, and after the many political meetings held in the rooms available for hire those attending them would also drink in the bar afterwards, hence earning it the nickname of the Communist Centre. New Years Eve celebrations were renowned, and it was essential to get there early to get a seat. Equally, Friday nights became a popular time to drink in the place and on occasions live music nights were on offer.

By 2005 the community centre had changed somewhat. There is still a bar, an arts group and Fusion, and various leisure activities operate from the centre such as dance classes and martial arts as well as a lunch club. A fashionable political theme developed in the 1990s termed "partnership", under which community projects were encouraged to join forces, and EOCC went into "partnership" with the Healthy Living Initiative (a government enterprise aimed to improve quality of life for vulnerable people in the community) at the end of the decade. As a result, there are some rather grand plans to add a kitchen on to the front of the EOCC to provide a new service in the centre. Undoubtedly a historic landmark, the old Cowley St. John Boys School has been radically altered and this has changed the landscape of the road. Sadly, there are very few original buildings of this nature left on the road.

THE ASIAN CULTURAL CENTRE

The Asian Cultural Centre has probably in some senses replaced the EOCC, as it provides a suitable venue for the activities that were accommodated in the centre in the 1970s and 1980s. A management committee is responsible for the running of the centre. Multi-cultural play schemes run during summer holidays for children aged between six and thirteen. There is also an Asian elders' club, a lunch club, water colour classes, Asian language courses, yoga classes and a karate club, and public meetings are also held there. The centre is housed in the pretty nineteenth-century chapel that was once part of the workhouse.

127

7

THE ROAD THAT NEVER SLEEPS: FROM THE ASSEMBLY ROOMS TO THE ZODIAC

Walk up Cowley Road most evenings, and you will see that the area is usually brimming with activity. There are people of all ages enjoying themselves in different ways, but there can be no mistaking that younger people are in the majority. Over the last fifteen years or so, Cowley Road has become a central point for youth culture in the city. As well as having a thriving restaurant and bar business, Cowley Road can also boast a flourishing music scene that has built up a national reputation. This chapter will look at musical events on Cowley Road from 1950 to today.

Cowley Road has never really been associated with classical music; Oxford's two major concert halls, the Sheldonian and the Holywell Music Room, are in the old city centre. The street's claim to fame has been much more based on popular music, but even this is a relatively recent phenomenon.

LIVE MUSIC IN THE 1960S

In the early 1950s, apart from tea dances at the Coop Hall, there was very little musical activity in Cowley Road, with most events taking place in central Oxford or the university. It is worth remembering that expectations regarding social life and music were radically different then, and young people filled their leisure time in other ways. Dances in the 1950s and 1960s were usually an event held on a Saturday night where both sexes went to in order to find a partner for courting. The bands that played at these dances were made up of local lads (it was usually men then) and the music was of a general nature. But by the late 1960s there were already the beginnings of an alternative social scene along Cowley Road, based mainly in pubs and around folk music.

Mainstream music concerts and dances, meanwhile, were still held in the city centre and reflected local demand for nationally known music. Adrian

Hopkins, an East Oxford resident, started to promote bands from outside the area in the early 1960s. Local bands also featured in these concerts, either as a supporting act or as the main promotion. Adrian started on this course of action because there was a demand for such entertainment and a gap in the market. He remembers one of his earliest ventures around 1963, when he put on a band in the town hall called Rocking Harvey and the Hayseeds from Nottingham. The Falling Leaves, a local band, were the supporting act for this event.

From then on Adrian promoted many successful events in the city, and more famous bands appeared, ranging from The Crazy World of Arthur Brown to Amen Corner. Other venues apart from the town hall were used for live music, such as Seacourt Tower in Botley and the Bridge Hotel at Wheatley. Adrian, who is still very much involved in the music business today, also used to organize coach trips to venues outside Oxford where up to half a dozen acts might perform.

A popular place for live music in the early to mid-sixties was The Forum in High Street, and local bands regularly played there. One such band was the Falling Leaves, who played as a supporting band with the Rolling Stones in 1964. University colleges would have summer balls that attracted top bands such as the Pink Floyd, and again local bands had the opportunity to play at these events, even though there was not the same abundance of local talent as there is today. Jazz clubs were also in existence in the city, and musicians such as Kenny Ball played to a mixed clientele of students and townspeople at Carfax Assembly Rooms on jazz nights.

SOLIDARITY MUSIC

When, during the 1970s, there was an upsurge in grass roots political activity, groups were formed to respond to national and international political struggles, such as the Chile Solidarity Campaign, the Oxford Palestinian Campaign and the Oxford Committee for Human Rights in Argentina. A pattern developed in relation to Cowley Road, whereby the long-established tradition of fundraising for political organizations and campaigning groups began to manifest itself in the new form of "benefits". Although these were held all over the city, the vast majority took place on Cowley Road, possibly because, as suggested earlier, many supporters lived in the area and there were suitable venues for musical events like the Coop Hall and East Oxford Community Centre. Both of these establishments were, broadly speaking, sympathetic to the politics of the different organizations.

Another favourite location for benefits and gigs was the Cape of Good Hope. Inevitably, local bands were asked to perform for benefits, which sometimes meant playing for free. Even if they did charge for performing, then this was still seen as furthering a cause they believed in. Given the number of political causes holding benefits, it was easy to believe that certain bands would never be able to make a living by playing. Discos were also becoming a lucrative and enjoyable way of raising money for groups. The Oxford Campaign for Homosexual Equality organized regular fundraising socials at East Oxford Community Centre in the mid-1970s. Other groups also cottoned on to this fundraising activity, and regular discos for political campaigns raised necessary funds and provided a social environment to further the cause.

Rock Against Racism (RAR) was influential in organizing gigs along Cowley Road in the late 1970s and early 1980s. Founded by a group of musicians and political activists belonging to the Anti-Nazi League in the mid-1970s, the aim of RAR was to unite musicians against racism and fascism, which had seemed to be growing in the form of right-wing organizations such as the National Front and British Movement. In April 1978, 100,000 people had marched through London's East End, where there was a strong National Front presence, to a Rock Against Racism concert in Victoria Park, Hackney. Punk rock and new wave bands were among the musicians involved in the fight against racism, and some of the top-name bands of the time who appeared at the carnival were X-Ray Spex, The Clash, Steel Pulse, and Tom Robinson. The movement sought through music to represent the multi-cultural interests of those interested in fighting racism and to attract young people within this environment.

In the first two months of 1980 there were three RAR events held in Cowley Road, at the EOCC, Coop Hall and the Cape of Good Hope. The local bands performing at these events were Criminal Damage, The Delta 5's, the Stereotypes and Alien Culture. Today the Anti-Nazi League campaigns under the name of Love Music Hate Racism.

SHOCK ROCK

At the same time as political struggles were intensifying, the local music scene was beginning to broaden out, with a new wave of alternative bands including punk rock and all-woman groups. Bands such as the Sex Pistols and the Stranglers led the way nationally with political messages in songs like "God Save the Queen" and "No More Heroes," while on a local level bands embraced these attitudes. The lifestyle of punks was attractive to many young

people, as it encouraged individualism, anarchy and a rejection of the establishment. A local man recalls his late teenage years living with his friends in a
squat on Cowley Road, and dedicating his life to creating and practising new
wave music. This was punctuated by breaks for snacks of baked beans and chips
in "Dirty Gertie's", otherwise known as the Crystal Snack Bar, a favourite café
of the time for all and sundry. The experience of this kind of lifestyle was salu-
tary for many as an expression of freedom and a rite of passage.

In the mid- to late 1970s the Oranges and Lemons in St. Clements, now
the Angel and Greyhound, was the place for punk bands to perform. John
Otway and Wild Willy Barrett were regular entertainers there. One local musician who was part of this cultural scene was Ken Liversausage, a.k.a. Dick Page,
an outrageous and popular performer. His stage performances were thoroughly entertaining and are a legend in themselves. Dick, who now lives in Ireland,
remembers this time with relish: "it was chaos!" Indeed, many who witnessed
his performances would probably agree, especially as he was known to com-
bine stunt performances with playing. The following memory from Dick
suggests just how exciting, volatile and anarchic his act was when he played in
the 1970s:

> Ken Liversausage started as a duo with one song then progressed to 11
> with 26 songs in an hour and was influenced by Zappa, the Tubes and
> cross dressing in various outrageous outfits. I used every prop I could—
> bikes to women, and "I don't give a fuck lyrics"… Lyrics were mainly
> about vomit, fucking up, shit and drugs! Soon began to take myself seri-
> ously… and seriously thought I was good… Punks and skinheads and
> bikers were the main followers and students… Shock Rock seemingly
> appealed to many, thanks to punk… Always tried to shock—matter of
> pride really. Had a punch up with Phil Collins and played to Pete
> Townsend and Sid Vicious in Speakeasy London. Fell through stage at first
> gig—had broken drumstick pushed into my arse while flashing to audi-
> ence—spent hours bent over bar having splinters removed by my
> landlady! Once the whole band was in full costume, off their heads in
> casualty after the roadie turned the van over after doing a gig in
> Wantage—no one hurt that bad but all staff keen to look and get auto-
> graphs—crazy!
>
> Gigs would often end up in a punch up… [there was a] high turnover
> of staff 'cos I thought I was God—no room for compromise there!
> Couldn't sing or play a note but thought I could. Biggest crowd was 3,500,

I wouldn't come off stage, so they pulled the plug and in the paper next day a police spokesman said, "if Mr Liversausage had used that sort of language on the street we would have been forced to arrest him." Split the ceiling in the Oranges and Lemons and my ears bled after playing too loud. 3,000 watts was a bit excessive, I suppose—200 was normal pub sound level but I liked it loud! Still do! I liked my backing vox to look like Roxy Music but they liked to dress in dustbin bags. Supported Generation X and Tubeway Army, and many other up-and-coming bands. £25 was normal pay but once got £100—a lot 30 years ago... my plan for every gig was to shock! I always ended up naked at the end! For the Jubilee celebrations I was the Queen in a wedding dress, crown and riding a mini motorbike round the Oranges and Lemons car park before making my first solo gig with the Robert Wakely Band and waved to the crowd...

To say that Dick enjoyed his career in the entertainment industry would be something of an understatement. If today he admits that he could neither sing nor play, there is no doubt that he pulled the crowds and was a talented entertainer. His antics, fuelled by alcohol, were encouraged by his audience who loved the unpredictability of the show. They were sometimes risky, as this recollection shows:

Did a gig at the Coop Hall and borrowed my mate's 1200 Harley Davidson bike, it was a beautiful bike. We had to do all sorts of things to get it up the back... made ramps and carried it up. Nobody knew what was going to happen... I burst through the fire doors on this bike... supported by two blokes...There was shock horror on the faces of audiences... it was difficult to steer the bike on the polished floor... and I picked up speed as I got towards the stage and tried to avoid crashing into the audience! The bike owner was horrified... the original plan was to ride round the room but this was not on as I could not control it!

One follower remembers: "The thing about Ken Liversausage was that he was so totally outrageous... he was a good floorshow... wild, unpredictable and very entertaining." Ken Liversausage was around for a relatively short time—probably just under two years—but he is well remembered as a performer whose behaviour was unconventional and often offensive, but never boring. As Dick says, "Thank God for punk, it gave everyone a chance to have a go, including me."

FROCK ROCK

Maeve Bayton was part of a 1970s Oxford women's band, the Mistakes. As well as being a musician, she has also carried out an extensive study of female popular music performers. She considers that punk created opportunities for more people to become active in the music business because the movement weakened the monopoly of the traditional male rock musician, allowing more women to become active in music.

Expectations of music and musicians changed, and it became more acceptable for women to play in bands, regardless of whether they played punk or not. Of course, men also benefited from this cultural shift because, as Ken Liversausage discovered, an extravagant and outrageous stage show could make up for a lack of conventional musical talent. Yet, in the case of all-women bands, there was inevitably a clash of cultures as some women performers had a strong feminist ethos that they projected in their music and lifestyles. Maeve recalls the atmosphere of the time and remembers playing gigs where audiences were made up of followers of the Mistakes and bands such as Ken Liversausage. Different bands inevitably played at the same events, but followers of the bands expected different things. Some expected an outrageous performance, while others wanted to listen to the music of the bands. Dick recalls that "everyone used to spit to show appreciation for your gig or throw beer cans... in a bizarre punk way." The Mistakes, for their part, were asked by some members of the audience to "show us your tits." The band had to learn to become resilient to this sort of sexist remark and behaviour, and some elements of the audience could be downright offensive towards the women, but for others sexism was unacceptable. This was an experimental time for popular culture and music, and the mixing of different bands at events represents how diverse the scene was. Attitudes towards women in general were beginning to change, yet old-fashioned values and reflexes were also persistent.

Alongside these developments was the founding of Mayfly, which started in 1973 and was a free alternative open-air concert held in Oxpens on May morning. Among the first local bands to play at the concerts were the Global Village Trucking Company and the Half Human Band. Some of the planning for subsequent concerts was planned in Uhuru. Mayfly has now become an established event. Back in the 1970s when the event was pioneered, fundraising gigs were organized featuring, among others, Ken Liversausage and the Mistakes. Other bands on the circuit then were Bongo Danny & the Enchanters, Institution, Acme Sewage and the Beast. Mayfly was a popular event for local people and was seen as a good live open-air experience.

Some pubs began to branch out and provide live music along Cowley Road. One in particular was the Bullingdon Arms, run by Joe Ryan. The "Bully" already had a reputation for Irish music, but during the 1980s the pub was extended to allow for bigger events and started to build a reputation on the circuit as it offered something of a nightclub atmosphere. Music was a mixture of live acts and DJs, and different types of sounds were offered, with Indie, retro, rock and jazz all having a place there. Later, when Joe took over the Elm Tree in the early 1990s, he also held similar events there. The Bullingdon continues to have a very active live music scene and has regular Blues nights which have become very popular.

FOLK MUSIC

Folk music has been part of the East Oxford music scene for a considerable time, with many folk musicians active in the Cowley Road area as well as in folk clubs in other parts of town such as Jericho and South Hinksey. In 1976 the East Oxford Folk Group was meeting regularly for ceilidhs at East Oxford Community Centre. The Half Moon was also a regular venue for folk music in the area, but when it closed for a while folk music moved temporarily to the Temple Bar, with a regular slot on Sunday lunchtimes, which was extended to Sunday evenings because it turned out to be a very popular event.

When Joe Ryan took over the Bullingdon Arms in 1977 he inherited many of the existing clientele from the Irish community, many of whom worked in the construction industry or the car factory. Local musicians were already established in the pub, and Joe, who came from an area in Ireland where live music was appreciated in pubs, encouraged performers. The Bullingdon came to be one of the most popular pubs on Cowley Road, largely because of its relaxed atmosphere and strong musical emphasis. By the 1980s the folk musicians had linked up with other live music acts in the Bullingdon, and as these events developed a reputation, it was not unknown for established musicians to "drop in". After Joe extended the Bullingdon he still kept the traditional folk music events.

According to some established folk musicians, there was a time (in the 1970s and 1980s) when Cowley Road was "the place for folk music". Ian remembers when "there wasn't a single pub where you couldn't go and sing a song on the Cowley Road." Folk music has since moved back to St. Clements, to the Port Mahon, where it has thrived for many years, and back to the Half Moon, where the landlord is now Joe Ryan.

VENUE SHORTAGE

Live music in the 1980s took place all over Oxford, but not principally on Cowley Road. Gigs were held at the Corn Dolly and Penny Farthing in town. The Caribbean Club, originally in Cowley Road in the mid-1970s, had by this time moved to South Oxford and also provided a regular venue for live music. There was also an upsurge in the clubbing scene, with places like Bogarts, Downtown Manhattan, Menzies, the Coven and Minchery Farm Country Club enjoying good custom. Besides this, there was a lot of musical activity in the Jericho area, mainly in the Radcliffe Arms and the Jericho Tavern, which had turned from a Beefeater pub into a music venue.

Once live music came on the circuit in Jericho, it created a precedent and Oxford began to get a reputation for hosting big bands. Another popular venue in Jericho was St. Pauls, now Freuds. Oxford Polytechnic, later Oxford Brookes University, was yet another place for gigs, as was Oxford College of Further Education at Oxpens and, occasionally, Oxford Town Hall.

In East Oxford, the Cape of Good Hope had a facility upstairs, the Point, which was used for musical events. Playing there was considered "a step in the up and coming direction". The Oranges and Lemons continued to host live music, while sporadic gigs were held in the Coop Hall during the 1980s. There were also the open-air free festivals in South Park that took place over several decades. Bands performing in Oxford during this time included the Crop Dusters, Levellers, Satan Knew My Father, Swerve Driver, Creation and a popular group, the Wild Poppies, who were based in East Oxford.

As the local music scene expanded, it became logical to write about and advertise it, and in 1986 a music paper, *Local Support*, was set up by Dave Newton, who previewed and reviewed events. By this time there were a considerable amount of local bands and, according to Dave, bigger venues were needed. The venues that could already hold larger audiences were the Town Hall, Oxford Polytechnic and the Coop Hall. But the Polytechnic had problems renewing its live music licence as residents were concerned about noise, and the Town Hall building structure was apparently unable to cope with the decibels generated by gigs. Consequently, these two venues were unable to continue providing regular live events from the mid-1980s onwards. Around 1994 venues in Jericho also became more restricted, and the Cape of Good Hope was no longer available for music. This left very few options to promote local bands at a time when there was a surge of creativity.

OXFORD ROCK

Oxford had produced only a handful of high-profile bands since the 1970s. One of the first was Mr. Big, quite prominent nationally from the early 1970s with chart hits, album releases and tours. There was something of a lull until the late 1980s, when Ride, comprised of four local lads from Oxfordshire, came to attention. Starting on the Oxford circuit in 1989 and playing at local venues such as the Jericho Tavern alongside other local bands, it was during a tour in 1990 as a supporting band to the Soup Dragons that the break came for Ride when a successful record promoter from Creation Records came to hear them play. When they were signed up for a record deal with Creation, their career took off, and as well as playing at local events they performed at the Reading Festival and other events with big name bands. Ride made several albums, went on national and international tours and were well received by the national music media. During the early 1990s Ride had successful tours in the United States, Australia, Japan and Europe.

One of the most significant aspects of Ride's route to fame was that they followed a local music circuit, and as their popularity increased they started to put Oxford on the music map. Oxford did not as yet have a national reputation for promoting good bands, but Ride began to change this perception as their popularity grew. Advertisements for Oxford-base events in the music media such as *New Musical Express* also added national publicity to the scene.

In the wake of the Ride success, another two local bands contributed to the impressive music scene that was developing fast and furiously in the early 1990s: Radiohead and Supergrass.

Radiohead, who were from Abingdon, have been together in some form since 1982. Their debut was at the Jericho Tavern in 1987, when they were known as On a Friday. By 1991 they were well integrated into the circuit, playing frequently at gigs, receiving reviews, an EMI contract and a name change to Radiohead. The band went from strength to strength and became nationally and internationally renowned. At this time, some of the band's members lived in East Oxford, and although they continued to support the local music scene, their following was so great that there was simply no venue big enough to accommodate the crowd that they would pull in.

A concert in South Park was held in 2001, billed as a fundraising event for local charities. The *Oxford Mail* reported on how the beneficiaries were to use their donations in September 2001:

Two Oxford charities are using cash donated from Radiohead's concert at South Park to move, while a third is giving its current base a facelift.

The £20,000 received by the Luther Street Night Shelter will go towards building a new night shelter on the current site. Work is expected to start next April. Oxford Samaritans will use their £20,000 donation to relocate to a new site in Magdalen Road. The move will be completed by the end of November.

A further £10,000 has been donated to the Mind Acorn Drop-in Centre, Barns Road, Cowley, which will use the money to carry out structural renovations and brighten up the centre, which works with people with emotional and mental health problems.

Radiohead's concert at South Park on July 7 raised £145,000 for 14 charities working in Oxfordshire.

Paddy O'Hanlon, director of the Night Shelter, said he was very pleased with the boost from Radiohead. "We have had a connection with them for several years," he said.

Spokesman for the Samaritans Mike Brown said the organisation was extremely grateful for the donation, which would cover about ten per cent of the organisation's move. The new building will be equipped with a lift and will improve access for disabled callers and volunteers.

The Orchestra of St John's, which played on Radiohead's last two albums and recorded with them at Dorchester Abbey, will also receive £20,000.

The remaining £75,000 will be divided equally between ten charities—Douglas House Hospice, Soundabout, Stonham Housing

Association, Oxford Wheels Project, Children in Touch, Undercurrents, Special Care Baby Unit, Asylum Welcome, Corporate Watch, Emmaus Oxford.

As a follow up to the concert, money raised went towards the publication of a book in June 2003 about the work of campaigners against the immigration detention centre, Campsfield House. The book, *Opening the Doors to Freedom*, has messages of support from the band, actress Dame Diana Rigg, poet Benjamin Zephaniah, and novelist Beverley Naidoo. An *Oxford Mail* article reported to its readers the support that Radiohead gave to the campaign:

> The Oxford charity, Asylum Welcome, which set up the Oxford Bail Support Group with money donated by Radiohead, has managed to secure the release of more than a hundred people held at Campsfield over the past three years. Asylum seekers held there while waiting for their appeals to be heard have no automatic right to bail and can be held indefinitely.
>
> A spokesman for Radiohead said: "We're proud that our music has helped provide funds so that the Oxford Bail Support Group can offer hope and liberation for some of those people unjustly imprisoned at Campsfield."

There are other causes that Radiohead have supported, and it is clear that a band that enjoys such status can make an enormous contribution to the community. While many other bands and performers who are not as well known have also made similar contributions and should not be overlooked, the case of Radiohead is inspirational.

Supergrass, another band made up of local boys, was formed in 1994. Two of the band members had been in the Jennifers, an earlier local band, before Supergrass was formed. After playing on the local circuit, Supergrass enjoyed national and international success. One of their first successful hits, "Caught by the Fuzz", is based on a personal experience of arrest by one of the band.

Although the band followed a similar route to Radiohead and Ride, Supergrass have their own culture and following. When the band took a break from touring to write a new album in 2002 and stayed in France for a couple of months, it gave them new impetus and, according to their official website, revived a very positive memory: "Being together in France felt just like the old days, when we all lived together on the Cowley Road (Oxford). The relaxed atmosphere pulled the band together and gave them an element of focus. It put them in a positive state of mind and created the vibe and energy that would set the tone for the album." Cowley Road, it seems, had a creative effect on Supergrass, especially as this was where they lived when they began their ground-breaking work.

Another band that got onto the national circuit around the same time as these very successful ones was the Candyskins, but unfortunately they never took off in the same way. Even so, it is important to recognize that not all local bands have to be ultra-successful in the traditional way, as many give much pleasure to the local community and keep the scene alive. The flourishing musical culture in Oxford was good reason for the beginnings of a regular new alternative music magazine in 1995, *Nightshift*. *Nightshift* was able to fill a gap by promoting, reviewing, advertising and coordinating the expanding local music industry, and continues to do so today.

THE ZODIAC

When Ride were launched on Oxford's local circuit, the available venues were limited to those in Jericho, the Cape of Good Hope, the Town Hall, the Coop Hall and the Apollo. The success of this band drew crowds that demanded bigger venues, and in general this was also a problem for other up-and-coming acts, let alone other touring bands and other musical events. In the early 1990s, the Coop Hall was transformed into a club for live music under the name of the Venue. In 1995 the place was reinvented as the Zodiac.

The Zodiac was a live music and club facility set on two floors with two stages, two bars and a cocktail bar and accommodated 700 people. This venture was the idea of Adrian Hicks and Nick Moorbath and had the backing of the successful Oxford bands, Ride, Supergrass and Radiohead. The success of these local bands and the promise of more talent meant that a serious place to perform was becoming essential. Just as important was the support that the Zodiac gave to the new local bands starting out, and this was recognized by those who had "made it" and wanted to encourage new performers. These bands continued to promote the Zodiac today in one way or another and effectively put back something into the community that had supported them.

The Zodiac was in many ways a gamble, but there was a lot of trust in Nick and Adrian from sponsors of the project, Supergrass, Ride and Radiohead. Their contacts and commitment to live music turned the Zodiac

into Oxford's most successful and renowned venue of this kind, reinforced by the three bands, which helped Oxford to develop a good music reputation. Over time the Zodiac also built its reputation, partly because of the calibre of the acts it attracted and partly because of a non-threatening atmosphere that encouraged people to frequent the place and spread the word. Acts that performed there came from across the music spectrum, from Courtney Pine and Robert Plant to Rage Against the Machine.

Nick maintained his contacts with big name bands which continued to perform at the Zodiac on a regular basis. He introduced a variety of club nights most evenings of the week, and the Zodiac provided for many different music interests ranging from Indie to dance and salsa and offered an alternative to the pub culture in the city centre. Benefit gigs were often held for organizations such as Oxfam. Despite alcohol being served there was relatively little trouble at the Zodiac, which Nick believed to be due to the sort of people who came and their expectations from an evening out.

The Zodiac has now been taken over by the Academy Music Group Ltd. and renamed the Carling Academy Oxford. The venue underwent a £2-million enlargement and refurbishment during the summer months of 2007, with three separate performance areas. Before its opening manager Carl Bathgate told the *Oxford Mail*: "I think it is the best 1,000-people capacity venue in the whole of the country." Now that the place has been refurbished top bands are expected to perform.

NATIONAL ATTENTION

The national media also picked up on the success of Oxford's music scene. In 1997 Oxford City hosted Radio 1's Sound City, giving local bands an opportunity to perform alongside big names on a national radio station broadcast. Soon afterwards, Channel 4 broadcast *Sounds of the Suburbs*, a documentary on Cowley Road's music scene, presented by John Peel. It looked at various artists in the area and presented a very encouraging picture of some unusual local talent. John Peel remarked that the "innovation and experimentation that go on [in the Zodiac] are equal to anything happening behind the hallowed walls of the university and possibly a lot more fun." He also described Cowley Road as "the very heart of Oxford's music." The programme confirmed what an original place Cowley Road was and the flattering overview was an accolade to those working in the business. John Peel also hinted at the breadth and depth of Oxford's contemporary music: "it has been said that there are more bands in Oxford per head of the population than anywhere else in Britain, though who said it history is not revealing."

CONCLUSION: THE NEXT FIFTY YEARS

Cowley Road's transformation from a traditional, conservative, predominately white area into a radical, multi-racial, environmentally conscious community has been a fascinating journey. The saga of the inner relief road had its influence on this process as it ensured that house prices remained lower than in other parts of the city. The legacy of planning blight may have helped create a "spontaneous bohemianism" not dissimilar to some parts of London, and with this came a tacit level of tolerance. Then, when people from different ethnic backgrounds and large numbers of students moved to the area, the atmosphere of tolerance and an "alternative" ethos were reinforced.

When I asked people for their impressions of Cowley Road for this book, the idea of tolerance was a common one. As one person put it, "there are some quite mad people around here, but nobody minds." There are, of course, pockets of intolerance and occasional tensions, but these are outweighed by liberal and relaxed attitudes. It is ironic that outsiders sometimes think of Cowley Road as a "No Go" area, but most people who know it find it safe.

In case I should be accused of looking through rose-coloured spectacles, it is worth issuing a word of caution. Much work and effort has been put into Cowley Road to improve life for different sections of the community. Attempts to make the street cleaner, safer and more aesthetically pleasing continue. But it might be argued that efforts of this sort, though worthy in them-selves, can perhaps be counter-productive and even lead to a more sanitized and artificial community. Might the ambition of cleaning up Cowley Road actually destroy the very atmosphere that was so appealing in the first place? "Spontaneous bohemianism" is not always compatible with urban regenera-tion. And because the area is already seen as attractive to live in, house prices are rising and people are being priced out of the market.

Since the first edition of this book there have been various developments on the road. It is encouraging that some property developers have listened to res-idents' concerns, as in the case of Ardant/W. E. Black partnership, which originally planned for student accommodation in the old Blackwell building but eventually sold the property to the Ethical Property Company (www.ethicalproperty.co.uk).

Major road works carried out in 2005 in the name of environmental and safety improvements have altered the appearance of Cowley Road, with new parking and speed restrictions. Legislation has also imposed smoking bans and extended licensing hours. Now not only are there piles of cigarette ends out-side bars and restaurants, but there are also many al fresco smokers, thus increasing noise levels. The Thames Valley police are now calling for CCTV on Cowley Road, as they claim that they are hampered in catching criminals without cameras. According to the *Oxford Mail* (27 September 2007), there were more than 900 recorded crimes in Cowley Road in the year to April 2007—more than in any other street or road in Oxford. A limit to the amount of bars allowed may reduce such problems.

Independent traders remain under pressure from rising rents and—more recently—from high-street chains (several small shops such as Jeremy's and Unikkii closed in 2006/7). One current of opinion considers that multina-tional companies such as Costa Coffee (which opened in the former Barclays Bank) are driving away smaller traders; others argue that choice and a pleasant consumer environment will encourage trade along the road. More positively, the Cooperative Society has recently returned to the road with a convenience store on the corner of Divinity Road. and a locally owned ice cream parlour is planned on the old Blackwell site.

Another factor is changing the area. More and more student accommo-dation is creeping into the area, consisting of purpose-built halls of residence and houses of multi-occupation. While most accept that the presence of students is an advantage, there is also a less positive dimension. In some side streets residents are beginning to feel overwhelmed by anonymity, as the transitory nature of student tenancy means that they do not become part of the community. Some long-term residents have even moved away, leaving houses to be filled with yet more short-term student tenants. If the process continues, it could have an effect on the overall community, with school rolls falling and other services affected.

For the time being, at least, Cowley Road is a successful and mostly harmonious mix of different ages, faiths and cultures. At a time when much is made about disharmony in communities, then Cowley Road has a lot to celebrate. The Carnival is a striking example of how it has changed from post-war austerity to multi-cultural creativity. Preparations for the Carnival involve businesses, residents and community groups—people from all the various backgrounds represented in the area. It has several functions: to make money, to promote harmony in the community, and to have some fun. In that sense, it is a microcosm of daily life on Cowley Road.

FURTHER READING

Akhtar, Miriam and Steve Humphries, *The Fifties and Sixties, A Lifestyle Revolution*. Oxford: Pan Macmillan, 2001.

Bayton, Mavis, *Frock Rock: Women Performing Popular Music*. Oxford: OUP, 1999.

Black, Jeremy, *Britain since the Seventies: Politics and Society in the Consumer Age*. London: Reaktion Books, 2004.

Black, Jeremy, *Modern British History since 1900*. London: Macmillan, 2000.

Bourdillon, A., *A Survey of the Social Services in the Oxford District II: Local Administration in a Changing Area*. Oxford: OUP, 1940.

Boylan, John, *Cowley Road Methodist Church Centre, Oxford: Centenary 1904-2004*. Oxford: Cowley Road Methodist Church Centre, 2004.

Briggs, Asa, *A Social History of England*. London: BCA, 1994.

Brown, Callum, *The Death of Christian Britain*. London: Routledge, 2001.

Bruley, Sue, *Women in Britain since 1900*. London: Macmillan Press, 1999.

Buchanan, Colin, *Traffic in Towns*. London: HMSO, 1963.

Butler, C.V., *Social Conditions in Oxford*. London: Sidgwick & Jackson, 1912.

Childs, David, *Britain since 1939, Progress and Decline*. Basingstoke: Palgrave (2nd edition) 2002.

Collins, Michael, *The Likes of Us: A Biography of the White Working Class*. London: Granta, 2004.

Collison, Peter, *The Cuttleslowe Walls, A Study in Social Class*. London: Faber and Faber, 1963.

Crossley, A., (ed.), *A History of the County of Oxford, Vol. IV, The City of Oxford*. Oxford: OUP, 1979.

Courtenay-Thompson, Frank, *Just By Chance: The Story of Marston Street and the Growth of an East Oxford Suburb*. Privately published, 1997.

Dibdin, Michael, *Dirty Tricks*. London: Faber and Faber, 1991.

Dummett, Ann, *A Portrait of English Racism*. Harmondsworth: Penguin, 1973.

Gibbs, Olive, *Our Olive, The Autobiography of Olive Gibbs*. Oxford: Robert Dugdale, 1989.

Graham, Malcolm, *On Foot in Oxford, 12. East Oxford*. Oxfordshire County Libraries, 1987.

Graham, Malcolm, *On Foot in Oxford, 3. St. Clements*. Oxfordshire County Libraries, 1987.

Graham, Malcolm, *Images of Victorian Oxford*. Stroud: Alan Sutton, 1992.

Hayter, Teresa and David Harvey (eds.), *The Factory and the City: The Story of the Cowley Automobile Workers in Oxford*. London: Mansell Publishing, 1993.

Hibbert, Christopher and Edward Hibbert (eds.), *The Encyclopaedia of Oxford*. London: Macmillan, 1988.

Honey, Derek, *Oxford: Beyond the University*. Witney: Affleck Press, 2003.

Horan, David, *Oxford: A Cultural and Literary Companion*. Oxford: Signal Books, (2nd edition) 2002.

Mogey, John, *Family and Neighbourhood: Two Studies in Oxford*. Oxford: OUP, 1956.

Newman, Roland, *The Oxford Inner Relief Road Controversy 1923-74, The Road and Christ Church Meadow*. Minster Lovell: Bookmarque Publishing, 1988.

Obelkevich, James and Peter Catterall (eds.), *Understanding Post-war British Society*. London: Routledge, 1994.

Panton, Andy, *Fare Stage for Bartlemas, A Personal History of the Cowley Road*. Privately published, 1986.

Parfit, Jessie, *The Health of a City: Oxford*. Oxford: The Amate Press, 1987.

Ponting, Lucie, *Public Health in Oxfordshire: The Past*. Oxford: Oxfordshire Health Authority, 1998.

Renton, David, *Red Shirts and Black: Fascism and Anti-Fascism in Oxford in the Thirties*. Oxford: Ruskin College Library, 1996.

Renton, David, *This Rough Game: Fascism and Anti-Fascism*. Stroud: Sutton, 2001.

Rose, Geoffrey, *A Pictorial History of Oxford City Police, 1869-1968*. Oxford: Oxford Publishing Co., 1979.

Rosen, Andrew, *The Transformation of British Life 1950-2000: A Social History*. Manchester: Manchester University Press, 2003.

Royle, Edward, *Modern Britain: A Social History 1750-1997*. London: Arnold (2nd edition) 1997.

Sharp, Thomas, *Oxford Replanned*. Oxford City Council, 1948.

Shatford, Susanne and Trevor Williams, *The Changing Faces of St. Clements and East Oxford, Books One and Two*. Witney: Robert Boyd Publications, 1997 and 1998.

Shaw, Alison, *Kinship and Continuity, Pakistani Families in Britain*. Amsterdam: Harwood Academic Publishers, 2000.

Sutton, Alan, *The Story of Oxford, A Short History of the City of Oxford*. Stroud: Alan Sutton Publishing, 1992.

Stump, Paul *The Music's All That Matters: A History of Progressive Rock*. London: Quartet Books, 1997.

Surman, Phyl, *Pride of the Morning, An Oxford Childhood*. Stroud: Alan Sutton Publishing, 1992.

Thornett, Alan, *From Militancy to Marxism: A Personal and Political Account of Organising Car Workers*. London: Left View, 1987.

Uhuru Collective, *Uhuru—A Working Alternative*. Oxford: 1975.

Waller, Robert, "Oxford Politics, 1945-1990", in R. Whiting (ed.), *Oxford, Studies in the History of a University Town since 1800*. Manchester: Manchester University Press, 1993.

Walton, H., *A Tree God Planted: Black People in British Methodism*. Ethnic Minorities in Methodism Working Group, 1985.

Whiting, Richard, "Association and Separation in the Working Class", in R.

Whiting (ed.), *Oxford, Studies in the History of a University Town since 1800.* Manchester: Manchester University Press, 1993.

Whiting, Richard, *The View from Cowley: The Impact of Industrialization upon Oxford 1918-1939.* Oxford: OUP, 1983.

Williams, Bridget, *The Best Butter in the World: A History of Sainsbury's.* London: Ebury Press, 1994.

Zweiniger-Bargielowska, Ina (ed), *Women in Twentieth-Century Britain.* Harlow: Longman, 2001.

DOCUMENTARY SOURCES

A Balanced Transport Policy—Report of Central Area Working Party to Council, 5 March, 1973.

City Council Reports

East Oxford Advertiser, 1970-1973

Kelly's Street Directories

Oxford Mail and *Times*

Radio Oxford Archives: Ref MT681 11/1971; MT683 11/71; MT108 3/11/74

Poster collection (from 1976)

USEFUL WEBSITES

www.strangeones.com (Supergrass)

www.ateaseweb.com (Radiohead)

www.corporatewatch.org.uk

www.eastoxford.com

www.asylum-welcome.supanet.com/whowe.html (Asylum Welcome)

www.ssmjchurchyard.org.uk (SS. Mary & John Graveyard Project)

www.dailyinfo.co.uk

INDEX